5 2007

EVERYTHING®

Guide to Being a
Personal Trainer

Dear Reader,

From the time we were young, we considered the gym our second home. We learned early on the importance of staying strong, fit, and healthy, and soon it became a way of life for us. We also had the privilege of witnessing firsthand the incredible changes in and growth of the fitness industry.

When we began working as personal trainers, neither of us knew it would end up being our full-time careers. Nor did we imagine how our careers would evolve into what they are today. (What kid thinks he will really get to work with the New York Yankees when he grows up?)

What began as a love for health and fitness has become so much more. Over the years, we have had the honor of training a diverse group of clients, who in turn have taught us valuable lessons about how to be successful in business and in life.

We undertook this project with the hope of teaching you how to achieve success in a fun and exciting industry. The information we share has taken us years to learn—through schooling, experiences, and mistakes. We hope that what you learn will help you enjoy the rewards of being a personal trainer as much as we do.

Kate Kenworthy   *Stephen Rodrigues*

The EVERYTHING Series

Editorial

Publisher	Gary M. Krebs
Managing Editor	Laura M. Daly
Associate Copy Chief	Sheila Zwiebel
Acquisitions Editor	Lisa Laing
Development Editor	Brett Palana-Shanahan
Associate Production Editor	Casey Ebert

Production

Director of Manufacturing	Susan Beale
Associate Director of Production	Michelle Roy Kelly
Prepress	Matt LeBlanc
	Erick DaCosta
Design and Layout	Heather Barrett
	Brewster Brownville
	Colleen Cunningham
	Jennifer Oliveira

Visit the entire Everything® Series at *www.everything.com*

THE

EVERYTHING®

GUIDE TO BEING A

PERSONAL TRAINER

All you need to get started
on a career in fitness

Kate Kenworthy, M.Ed., A.T.C., C.S.C.S. and
Stephen A. Rodrigues, M.Ed., P.E.S.

Adams Media
Avon, Massachusetts

We would like to dedicate this book to our clients as an expres-sion of our gratitude for their trust and devotion over the years.

An Everything® Series Book.
Everything® and everything.com® are registered trademarks of F+W Publications, Inc.

Published by Adams Media, an F+W Publications Company
57 Littlefield Street, Avon, MA 02322 U.S.A.
www.adamsmedia.com

ISBN 10: 1-59869-227-5
ISBN 13: 978-1-59869-227-3

Printed in Canada.

J I H G F E D C B A

Library of Congress Cataloging-in-Publication Data
available from the publisher.

This publication is designed to provide accurate and authoritative information with regard to the subject matter covered. It is sold with the understanding that the publisher is not engaged in rendering legal, accounting, or other professional advice. If legal advice or other expert assistance is required, the services of a competent professional person should be sought.
    —From a *Declaration of Principles* jointly adopted by a Committee of the American Bar Association and a Committee of Publishers and Associations

Many of the designations used by manufacturers and sellers to distinguish their products are claimed as trademarks. Where those designations appear in this book and Adams Media was aware of a trademark claim, the designations have been printed with initial capital letters.

This book is available at quantity discounts for bulk purchases.
For information, please call 1-800-289-0963.

Visit the entire Everything® series at *www.everything.com*

Contents

Top Ten Reasons to Become a Personal Trainer

1. Personal training is a fun, exciting, and high-energy profession.

2. You can positively impact your clients' well-being.

3. Personal trainers get to work with a diverse group of people with a variety of needs.

4. You'll receive satisfaction from helping people set and reach their goals.

5. There is creativity in almost every aspect of the business.

6. The field of personal training is continuously changing and growing.

7. Work schedules are flexible.

8. You'll have unlimited career growth-potential.

9. Personal trainers have the option of running their own business.

10. There is an opportunity to make a significant income.

Acknowledgments

We would like to thank:

Our friend "Mo," for being the impetus for this project and for believing in our abilities not only as personal trainers, but also as writers;

David Morin, for allowing us to develop our craft working as independent trainers in his health club; and

Kamran Khan, C.P.A., for consulting with us on the sections of this book related to accounting.

Kate would like to thank:

Coach Rod, for giving me my first personal training job, my career, and my life.

My daughter, Victoria, for helping me understand what is really important, and for being my assistant coach.

My mom, who taught me through both word and example how to set goals and aim high.

My family: Kevin, Scott, Ben, Auntie Gail, Uncle Ro, and Ta, for their unwavering love and support.

Tess and Alie, for being the world's best babysitters and for dropping everything to help me during crunch time.

Michael Zarli (my other big brother), who took me to the gym for the first time and got me hooked.

Maria Hutsick, for convincing me to become certified as a Strength and Conditioning Specialist and introducing me to functional training.

Stephen would like to thank:

My mom and dad, for teaching me the importance of hard work, discipline, and commitment. Also for believing in and supporting me in my endeavors over the years. I love you!

My brothers, Carl and David, for teaching me never to give up and being there when I need them most.

Jay Sears (my friend and first employee), for working to help further my career.

Keith, Tom, and Nelson, my childhood friends. Thanks for the memories and for your willingness to help with all of my special projects.

Peter Zeiger, for being a friend and mentor during my beginning years and believing in my skills as a personal trainer.

Dan and Kathy Sullivan, for their business advice and for helping me realize my dreams of owning and operating my own training facility.

Dave Salvadore, my client-turned-friend and confidant. Thanks for all the fatherly advice.

To my longest clients, Ed and Donna M. Thank you for your loyalty over the years, and I look forward to working with you for many more.

Introduction

Since the beginning of civilization, people have tried to improve their physical condition through training. Just look back to the ancient Greeks. From a young age, the Trojans would use training techniques to develop their soldiers into elite warriors. The Greeks also trained for and participated in the first Olympic games. Training methods have advanced in many ways due to research and technology, but fundamentally, they really have not changed all that much.

What has changed is the professionalism associated with training. Gone are the days when you learned how to work out from your friend who had been doing it longer. Or when the trainer at the gym was the guy who had won some competitions, and could help you bulk up, too. Personal training has evolved into a respectable, lucrative profession, and is now one of the fastest-growing careers.

As recently as the early nineties, personal training was considered a luxury. Fifteen years later, personal training is an industry generating over $4 billion a year in revenue, and that number continues to rise exponentially. As people become increasingly aware of the need for regular exercise, there is a growing demand for qualified, well-trained personal trainers.

With the rising demand for personal trainers comes an increased need for trainers who are qualified to work with special populations.

While personal trainers were once found only in health clubs and gyms working with healthy adults, you can now find them in a variety of settings working with diverse populations. Personal trainers are creating niches working with children, pregnant women, post-rehabilitation patients, people with chronic disease, and the elderly. And these are only some of the markets available to personal trainers. However, many people continue to view personal trainers as people who work in fitness centers. This book will provide you with a thorough understanding of what it takes to become a successful personal trainer, as well as the numerous opportunities that are available to you.

Many people who become personal trainers are unable to achieve the success they strive for. One major reason for this failure to thrive is that they lack the knowledge and skills that would set them apart from the average trainer. Another is that they neglect to look at personal training as a legitimate business. Running a successful business requires an understanding of sales, marketing, advertising, and much more. In order to create and maintain a profitable career, you'll need the proper tools. This book will explain what those tools are, why they are important, and how to acquire them. Whether you're just beginning your career or have been a personal trainer for years, this information will show you how to take advantage of the rapidly growing market and move ahead in this exciting career.

Chapter 1

Is Personal Training for You?

It used to be that a personal trainer was the big guy in the gym—Joe Bodybuilder—who had been there for years and decided to make money trying to help people look like him. While that scenario may still play out in some places, personal training as a whole has evolved, and continues to evolve, into a more reputable field. Most personal trainers are now considered to be health and wellness professionals. They go by many titles, including Fitness Consultant, Strength and Conditioning Specialist, Fitness Instructor, and Personal Fitness Coach.

Why Become a Personal Trainer?

Most people who become personal trainers do so because they feel passionately about being active, fit, and healthy, and want to teach others what they know. For these individuals, sitting at a desk for eight or more hours a day would be unbearable torture. As personal trainers, they're able to be social and on-the-go during a typical work day.

Becoming a successful trainer takes many long hours of developing your skills and your own personal training philosophy. Do not sacrifice learning and experiencing everything you can within the industry in order to make quick money. Over time, as your knowledge and skills grow, you'll be able to command more money.

Doing a Job You Love

It is rare to find someone who says sincerely that they love their job. In this profession, however, it's far less rare than in most. Personal trainers as a group tend to be vibrant, active, energetic, healthy people who love that they can be paid to remain that way. Being a personal trainer is fun and rewarding, and it challenges the mind and body in exhilarating ways. It can also be a very lucrative profession for those who do it well.

A Growing Industry

The health and wellness industry is growing exponentially. People are living longer and are becoming more aware of the importance of being physically fit throughout their lives. However, improvements in technology over the years have created a world where human beings don't need to be physical in their daily lives. With the advent of the personal computer and the Internet, people have everything they need at their fingertips. You no longer have to leave your house to shop for groceries, clothes, furniture, or any other necessities. You simply sit at your computer, type a few keys, and everything you need is delivered to your doorstep. Today, most people must actually make time to be active outside of work and the home.

 Fact

The U.S. Department of Labor predicts that the demand for personal trainers will increase by 46 percent over the next six years. This will cause the profession to be ranked one of the fifteen most desirable fields in which to work. If you begin your career now, you can be a part of this tremendous growth opportunity.

Each year, there is a growing number of fitness facilities being built and opened to fulfill the increasing demand for recreational exercise. As the number of health clubs, gyms, and studios increase, so does the demand for personal trainers to staff them. This tremendous growth is predicted to continue for some time, guaranteeing job opportunities for people in the industry.

Defining a Personal Trainer

Simply put, a personal trainer is a coach and an educator. A trainer teaches people how to set their fitness goals, and then coaches them toward achieving those goals. This is an extensive process during which a trainer wears many hats.

Motivator

The majority of your clients will see you between one and eight times per month. They are usually motivated enough to work out on their own, but they need a guide to encourage them. Your job is to help the client set goals, and then monitor her progress. Throughout this process, you need to give positive feedback and constructive criticism. There will be ups, downs, and plateaus, so you must teach your client what to do and coach her through the tough times when she needs a little extra inspiration and encouragement.

E ssential

Being able to keep your clients motivated is one of the most important factors in retaining them as clients. People are not likely to pay $50 an hour for your services if they don't feel like they're accomplishing something.

At the other end of the spectrum are clients who will hire you three or more times per week because they lack the motivation to exercise on their own. Knowing they have an appointment with you forces them to work out. For these people, you are the primary motivation. Goal setting and testing is just as important for this group as it is for your other clients, but you personally play a bigger role in helping them achieve their goals. If these clients want you to hold their hands, do it. At least they are being active. Not everyone has the same motivational drive, and as a trainer you need to accept that fact and work with it.

Nutritional Consultant

Obviously, most trainers are not registered dieticians (RDs). However, proper nutrition is vital to the success of any program, whether it be for weight loss, weight gain, athletic performance, or just general wellness. Therefore, it's important for trainers to be comfortable discussing at least the basics of nutrition. Ideally, a trainer has the knowledge to safely and effectively develop nutritional programs. This knowledge may be obtained through college courses and workshops. If you don't have this ability, you should at least have a referral system in place so you can send your clients to an RD who shares your health and wellness philosophies.

E ssential

It is called *personal* training for a reason. As a trainer, you can become very close with your clients. You need to know where the line is between being professional and being a friend. The line can become fuzzy, especially as you work with someone over a long period of time.

Friend/Confidant

It is important for your clients to like and trust you, not only so they continue to hire you, but so that you can more effectively help them reach their goals. In order to overcome your clients' fitness obstacles, you must know what the obstacles are, and you will only obtain that knowledge by getting to know your clients well. Many of your clients will train with you for months or even years. You'll see them through all kinds of life changes: marriage, pregnancy, childbirth, divorce, job changes, etc. These circumstances are both positive and negative stressors. Peoples' exercise routines and habits are affected by stress, as are their eating habits. The more aware you are of what is going on at any given time in their lives, the easier it will be to avoid or overcome pitfalls.

Business Person/Entrepreneur

As a personal trainer, you're running a business. Whether you're actually self-employed or working in a health club, you must have good business practices or you won't reach your full potential. If you have experience in business, you have a tremendous advantage. If you do not, it would be wise to take a course or two in this area. Taking a class in marketing or basic business administration will help you learn the fundamentals. Talking to established personal trainers who can act as mentors in this area is also helpful.

Traits of a Successful Personal Trainer

Personality plays a large role in whether or not a trainer is successful. People will start, and continue to work, with someone they enjoy being around. While you must also have the knowledge and skills to accompany these traits, it's true that a little personality goes a long way.

Leadership

Leadership is the ability to guide, direct, or influence people. A personal trainer must be able to lead clients in the direction they need to go and instill in them the desire to follow. The trainer's goal is to influence the client to change his harmful behaviors, many of which are lifelong, so he can be healthier and feel better. This is a great challenge and is virtually impossible for the trainer who coddles instead of leads.

Discipline

Living a healthy lifestyle requires a great deal of discipline. In today's world, there are fast food restaurants on literally every corner, and when a person does choose to avoid fast food chains and go into a real restaurant, the portion sizes are two to four times larger than they should be. The fact is, people work too much, eat too much, and spend too much time sitting in their cars and at their desks. Temptation is everywhere, and people are rarely encouraged to make good, healthy choices.

If you expect your clients to commit to being healthy, you must show them how to do it by your own example. You need to get enough sleep, eat well, and exercise regularly. You must live what you preach, not only to gain your clients' respect, but to demonstrate that it can be done.

Alert

Being aware of your personality strengths and weaknesses is crucial to your success. Everyone has flaws, but working on your weaknesses will assist you in gaining and retaining clients. It's helpful to talk to people you've worked for and with in an effort to learn more about your specific strengths and weaknesses.

Empathy

As a trainer, you are asking people to do some very difficult things. They are trying to break ingrained habits, and fit workouts into already full days. They may feel overwhelmed, embarrassed, or discouraged. It's important to let your clients know that you understand where they're coming from. You must be able to help people move outside of their comfort zone in a firm yet compassionate manner. Being condescending will only make a client feel more discouraged, and they'll be less likely to continue to work with you. They may even give up on fitness altogether.

Professionalism

Personal trainers have evolved from gym rats into fitness professionals. You may also have other professional people as your clients. Your clients are spending their valuable time and significant amounts of money to meet with you. For these reasons, it is important to present yourself in a professional manner. This means dressing appropriately, arriving on time for your appointments, and treating your clients and coworkers with respect. Another aspect of being professional involves making your policies and standard operating procedures (SOPs) clear from the beginning. Put them in writing and require a signature from your clients.

E ssential

Having your clients sign written policies for situations such as tardiness or no-shows will reduce confusion and possible conflict. Clients should be clear on what to expect if they miss an appointment or cancel at the last minute. Discussing these situations beforehand will also show your clients that you are prepared and professional.

Creativity

While it would be easy to take your routines from a book using a one-size-fits-all attitude, this isn't what personal training is about. Your job is to help your clients reach their potential by developing and implementing exciting routines and programs tailored to them as individuals. What motivates one person will not necessarily motivate another. People also differ greatly in the types of workouts they enjoy and can fit into their schedules. Therefore, you must use your creativity and imagination to keep each client interested and on the right path with diet and exercise. Your most difficult task won't be encouraging good routines, it will be developing creative methods to keep your clients motivated, interested, and focused to achieve their goals. You'll use your creativity in every aspect of your business.

Social Skills

Successful personal trainers tend to be extroverts. An outgoing personality will help you obtain and retain clients. Few people want to spend an hour working out with someone with whom they cannot have a conversation. It's helpful to learn about what your client does for a living and their hobbies. As time passes and you build trust and rapport, she may divulge more personal information that will help you better assist her in meeting her goals. In addition, the more she enjoys your company, the more she'll look forward to your sessions, and refer you to other people.

Ask open-ended questions to promote conversation. Open-ended questions are those that prompt more than a simple yes or no response, such as, "What do you feel is your biggest deterrent to exercise?" The more open-ended questions you ask, the easier it will be to get your clients talking and discover what makes them tick.

Skills of a Successful Personal Trainer

Personal trainers have varying amounts of experience and education. Some may call themselves trainers, yet they have no formal education. Others hold a graduate degree in exercise science. There are currently no legal standards or licensure requirements for personal trainers. No law states that people must do x, y, and z in order to call themselves personal trainers. There are, however, skills you should acquire before becoming a personal trainer.

E ssential

New clients have the best intentions of achieving their goals. Sometimes their excitement may cloud their impression of how much time they'll dedicate to exercise. When developing your programs, remember to keep them short enough to fit into busy schedules. Short workout schedules will be more manageable for your clients, and will increase the likelihood that they'll stick with them.

Program Design

Program design, also called exercise prescription or design, is a fitness plan you develop for your client. It must take into account factors such as fitness level, personality, and current and desired lifestyles. With proper program design, you'll help your clients achieve their goals in a safe and effective manner. A good program is one that is challenging but maintainable and enjoyable for your client. While you'll learn a great deal about program design from books, it's your ability to understand your clients that will help you the most in this area.

Sales

Personal training is a people business. That being said, it is still a business. Therefore, you must have good business skills or you will not be successful. While you don't have to be the stereotypical salesperson, you do have to sell yourself. This is a skill that can be learned and must certainly be practiced.

Part of being a good salesperson is your accessibility to potential clients. You need to be open and friendly, but not fake. You should always have a smile on your face, as it makes you more approachable. Be sure to make casual conversation with members in your facility, and learn names and pertinent information about as many people as possible so they feel comfortable approaching you to train them.

Career Opportunities and Income Potential

In this profession, your career opportunities and income potential are limited only by your ambition, imagination, and drive. Once you have the necessary education and experience, you can accomplish many goals, including writing books or magazine articles, making DVDs, starting an online business, or using your skills to start programs within the community. You could also open your own facility specializing in whatever area interests you. If you're willing to take risks and work hard, you can create an amazing career for yourself.

Places of Employment

There are many settings in which a personal trainer may work. The two most common are health clubs and gyms. Other popular settings include corporate fitness and personal training studios. Some personal trainers choose to travel to their clients' homes or run outdoor programs for their clients. While this book won't focus on them, there are some less common places that employ personal trainers, such as country clubs, spas, resorts, and cruise ships. Chapters 2–6 will discuss the most common places of employment in greater detail.

Income

Many trainers are well compensated for working with clients. Trainers typically command an hourly wage of $20–$100, with the average being $50 per hour. Factors that play a role in how much you can charge include: experience, education, type of clientele, geographic location, facility you work in (health club, studio, spa), and market rate in your area.

Geographic location plays a big role in how much you can charge for your services as well. Generally, trainers working in large cities can demand more for their services than those working in small cities. Cost of living, competition, and demographics must be considered when determining your pay scale.

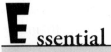

Bear in mind that because you're working with people in a physical way, there is always a risk of injury to the client. The more knowledge you have of human anatomy and physiology, the better you'll be able to prevent injury. You'll also be more qualified to work with populations who are already dealing with injury or illness.

Becoming a Personal Trainer

The first steps to becoming a personal trainer are ensuring you have the proper education and taking a certification exam. If you're currently working in or have a degree in a health or wellness profession, the transition into personal training should be fairly simple. You probably already have most or all of the knowledge you need to obtain a certification, and you'll simply require some on-the-job instruction and experience. If you're currently working in an unrelated field and would like to become a personal trainer, you should go through some type of formal education. This training isn't required by law, but will make you a much better trainer.

Education

There are many benefits to becoming educated before beginning your career. When you have a formal education, you are better prepared and qualified to assist your clients. Good personal trainers are proficient in the areas of human anatomy, exercise physiology, nutrition, psychology, and business. It's difficult to be successful if you're lacking in one of these areas. While this may seem like a lot of knowledge to acquire, it is attainable, and can be accomplished in a variety of ways.

In making a decision regarding education, you must first decide if you want to obtain a degree. You need to consider whether you have the time, money, and ability to go this route. A degree is a big commitment, and not something to be taken lightly. It is, however, a very prudent path to take as it will increase your job opportunities and earning potential.

If you do decide to attend a college or university, you must decide which one and what major to pursue. People who become personal trainers commonly major in exercise science, human movement, or physical education. These degrees will give you a good foundation in how the human body works, but you'll need to supplement your knowledge with courses or workshops more specific to the profession.

 Fact

Collegedata.com is a good resource for finding a college or university offering degrees or courses in your area of interest. While exploring their site, you may limit your search based on factors such as cost, location, and size of the school. This will help you focus and make your decisions on where to apply less overwhelming.

Because personal training is becoming so popular, colleges and universities have created majors designed specifically for personal trainers. This major is usually called something along the lines of health and fitness, and will have both academic instruction and hands-on experience. This type of degree is ideal but not essential.

Alert

A trainer cannot become proficient by taking a home-study or weekend crash course. If you lack a degree in a related field, consider taking a human anatomy course to better understand the human body. You can become a good personal trainer with only a certification, but education will help you develop into a great personal trainer.

If you choose not to obtain a degree, you must at least go through some type of training before becoming certified. You may consider taking a few college courses such as anatomy, biomechanics, nutrition, business, and sports psychology. Another option is to attend seminars and workshops presented by reputable organizations, such as those listed at the end of this chapter, designed to teach people to become personal trainers.

Certification

Even if you currently have or are working toward a degree, you should also become certified. Certification is simply credentialing that ensures you are minimally competent in key areas before you begin your career. There are currently over seventy-five certifications available for personal trainers, and the numbers are continually increasing. However, only a small number of these certifications and certifying bodies are legitimate. To further complicate matters, many organizations offer more than one type of certification. You must choose an organization through which to become certified, as well as the type of certification you'd like to receive.

There are numerous factors to consider when choosing an organization through which to obtain certification. First and foremost, the organization should have high standards for certification and continuing education. One way to ensure that you're making a good choice is to choose an organization that has been accredited by an unbiased third party. The main agency responsible for accreditation is the National Organization for Competency Assurance (NOCA). NOCA "develops standards and accredits organizations that meet them." Applying to NOCA for accreditation is a voluntary process. Organizations are put through a rigorous process to ensure they meet high standards. You can visit their Web site at *www.noca.org* and search their member directory to find out if your certifying agency is accredited. You can also check your agency's Web site. If they are accredited, they will say something about NOCA or NCCA, which is the accreditation body of the NOCA.

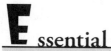

The field of personal training is not currently regulated by federal or state governments. While physical therapists, athletic trainers, massage therapists, and even hair stylists are required to be licensed by the Board of Health, personal trainers are not. This is unfortunate, as it would standardize and add credibility to the profession. It's likely, however, that in the next decade there will be licensure requirements.

If for some reason the organization you wish to use is not accredited, they should at least be recognized by IHRSA and require their members to complete continuing education to maintain their skills. A simple online certification isn't adequate, and could set you up for failure, or even legal problems in the future.

The following is a list of ten certifying agencies (along with their web addresses) that you may explore in your journey to becoming a personal trainer. All ten are at least minimally reputable, but it is up to you to decide whether or not they meet your own standards and needs.

1. American College of Sports Medicine (ACSM)
   www.acsm.org
2. National Strength and Conditioning Association (NSCA)
   www.nsca.com

3. National Academy of Sports Medicine (NASM)
   www.nasm.org
4. American Council on Exercise (ACE)
   www.acefitness.org
5. Aerobics and Fitness Association of America (AFAA)
   www.afaa.com
6. National Federation of Personal Trainers (NFPT)
   www.nfpt.com
7. National Council on Strength and Fitness (NCSF)
   www.ncsf.org
8. International Sports Sciences Association (ISSA)
   www.issaonline.com
9. American Fitness Professionals & Associates (AFPA)
   www.afpafitness.com
10. National Exercise and Sports Trainers Association (NESTA)
    www.nestacertified.com

The first three organizations have the highest standards for certification, but a certification from any of the ten listed would be adequate for you to get started. Once you've decided which certification exam to take, you may consider taking one or more workshops offered by the certifying organization in order to properly prepare. These workshops can be expensive, but are definitely worth your time and money. Unless you choose a home-study course, you'll be receiving important hands-on experience and instruction.

Once you've become certified, you should spend some time observing experienced trainers. It's helpful to shadow as many different people as possible in order to experience a variety of philosophies and techniques. It's also helpful to observe trainers in a variety of work settings, so you can experience what it's like to work in different environments with different populations. By doing this, you may get a feel for what type of setting you wish to work in, as well as with whom.

Chapter 2

Health Clubs and Gyms

Health clubs are, for the personal trainer, virtual playgrounds in which to acquire and train clients. In this setting, there lies a reservoir of potential new clients as well as tremendous resources. Clubs are a great place to learn the business and establish a reputation and clientele. Employees receive training in all areas of the business, and have the benefit of working with and learning from trainers who have more experience. That's why the majority of people just beginning their personal training careers will start in this setting.

Benefits of Training in a Club

Working in a health club setting provides personal trainers with a great many resources and experiences with which to develop their skills and expertise.

 Fact

In 2001, the International Health, Racquet & Sportsclub Association (IHRSA) estimated there were 17,807 clubs in the United States generating $12.2 billion in revenue. By 2005, there were approximately 26,831 health clubs generating $14.8 billion in revenue. That's $2.6 billion of growth in less than five years, and represents tremendous opportunities for fitness professionals.

Equipment

First and foremost, the exercise equipment in health clubs is typically state of the art. Every year new research brings about the development of better equipment, and the clubs that remain competitive are those that stay abreast of the rapidly changing technology. In addition to helping clubs attract new members, better equipment also helps the clubs retain their current members who are paying top dollar, and therefore expect the best.

Having new equipment at your disposal can be a great asset. It will allow you to keep your personal training appointments fun and exciting for both you and your clients, and help your clients reach their goals more quickly. This is only true, however, if you have the knowledge required to safely and effectively use the equipment and demonstrate proper use to your clients. It is critical to know the equipment inside and out, not only to properly help your clients, but also to avoid injuring them.

E ssential

Reading professional journals will help keep you abreast of the newest exercises and equipment on the market. Attending trade shows and seminars is also an excellent way to keep your knowledge current, as well as an opportunity to try new equipment.

Of all the settings in which a personal trainer may be employed, health clubs typically have the best variety of equipment. This is important because not only does it prevent boredom for your clients, it also gives you experience working with a wide range of cardio and weight training machines. Some cardio equipment you may see in a health club includes:

- Treadmills
- Ellipticals
- Crosstrainers

- Ergs (rowing machines)
- Stationary bikes
- Recumbent bikes
- Stairclimbers
- Arc trainers
- Upper-body bikes (UBEs)

A good trainer is able to use and explain each piece of equipment safely and effectively.

Experience Dealing with a Variety of Personalities

Your interactions with members/clients are priceless. While a formal education is important in becoming a personal trainer, it is your personal experiences that shape you as a trainer. Health clubs are a great place to learn the fitness business and establish yourself, because you encounter so many different types of people and situations. You'll also be able to observe and work with people who have varying fitness levels and knowledge of a gym.

Many clubs offer complementary training appointments to new members so they can learn the equipment. Many of these appointments will be with people who have never used weight or cardio machines before, and have possibly never even been inside of a gym. For these members, you need to keep things simple, straightforward, and enjoyable. You might also work with people who have been going to the club for years but are looking for a new program. For these people, you will need to get more creative. Depending on your club's policies, you may work with individuals as young as eleven and as old as eighty. You may possibly even work with people who have disabilities or injuries that make exercise modification a necessity. The greater the variety of people you work with, the more you'll learn.

Other Employees as Resources

Another benefit of working in a club is that you have other personal trainers as resources. There is a good chance that when you start working at a club, there will be at least a few people there with more experience than you. While there is no substitute for your own experiences, being able to learn from someone else's is also help-ful. Try to find mentors who are willing to share their experiences with you. It's important to inquire about what they think makes them successful in this setting, and what they've found to be ineffective. Developing a rapport with other trainers can help you be more successful at approaching new clients, selling training packages, discovering new training methods, retaining clients, and hopefully making a lasting career for yourself. Even if you've been a trainer for some time, there is always room to learn from others in the business. Keep in mind that each setting is different, and the tactics that may work in one setting won't necessarily help you be successful in other settings. So always remain open to changes and suggestions.

E ssential

Not only will people vary in their skills and abilities, they'll also have vastly different personalities. Some people you interact with will be easygoing and others will be difficult and demanding. You'll learn quickly the importance of patience and professionalism, as well as the value of keeping your members happy.

Choosing a Club to Work In

While health clubs and gyms make up one type of work setting, there is a great variation between each individual club. The type of work environment differs greatly from one club to the next, depending on factors such as size, location, management, hours, pay, and job requirements. Therefore, there is much to consider when looking for a position.

On-the-Job Training

A good health club has management that adequately trains its employees. Receiving proper training will greatly increase your success, and therefore, your income. Unfortunately, not every club gives proper training, and few do it well. If the club expects you to sell memberships, training packages, and/or nutritional supplements, they should have a standard sales presentation. If you're going to work the desk in the fitness center, you should be trained in how to use the computer system and how to educate new members on the equipment, as well as any other policies and procedures applicable to your club.

Deciding if the Club Fits You

There are many other factors to consider in choosing a place to work. What are the educational requirements for personal trainers? Some clubs require only that their trainers be certified. Some require a specific certification and others require a college degree. You will need to consider whether you have or are willing to obtain the education required for the job. If you meet or surpass the necessary requirements, consider whether or not the club's educational standards are high enough for you. Your reputation is influenced by the environment in which you work.

You must also consider whether or not there are bonuses, pay raises, and room for advancement. If you're interested in management, is it a possibility at this club? Do you receive bonuses for selling memberships and packages? How the club pays you for personal training appointments is also important. Some clubs pay a flat rate; others use a split such as 50/50 or 60/40. Other clubs use a sliding pay scale, such as 50/50 for up to twenty sessions per week and 60/40 for anything over twenty sessions. Will you always be at the same split, or will the percentages change over time? If you have a base salary, will it increase? Are benefits included, and if so, to what degree? The answers to these questions will vary widely from club to club. There are no right or wrong answers, only what is favorable to you and your desired lifestyle.

Another major factor to consider is the type of schedule you'll be working. Unlike many businesses, most clubs are open early and remain open late. Some are even open twenty-four hours. It is important to know when you are expected to be there and if those expectations fit your lifestyle. Some clubs schedule your personal training sessions for you, while others allow you to make your own appointments. You may be covering the desk in the fitness center and taking members through appointments at the same time. Or you may have a certain number of hours to cover the desk, and the rest of the time you are able to conduct personal training sessions.

Potential Clientele

When you hear the words potential client, does your mouth water? If it doesn't, it should. Clients equal money, and more clients mean more money and a better lifestyle. If you wish to be successful, you have to be hungry. You must always be thinking about how to get more clients, as well as how to keep the clients you already have. Do not expect your club to simply hand you clients. While this may happen to a small degree, you as a trainer must go out and sell yourself.

Obtaining New Clients

Members won't generally hire trainers they don't know. It's rare for someone to simply walk in off the street, sign up as a member, and ask for a personal trainer. This does occasionally happen, but you cannot build a successful business by relying on that scenario. People must know and trust you before they invest their time and money in you. Visibility is important. Let members get to know you (and you them) by walking around the fitness center and talking to people during your desk hours and/or between appointments.

 Question

How do I approach a potential client to sell my services as a personal trainer?
Establish a relationship by learning his name and finding things you have in common. Do not try to close a sale the first time you meet someone. The next time you see him working out, remember his name and explain what you do. You may have several conversations with someone before they feel comfortable enough to make an appointment with you.

There is one situation where you are more likely to sell an appointment to someone you have just met. When a new member joins a club, they are typically entitled to at least one free appointment with a trainer. You should use this as an opportunity to make your presentation and sell your personal training services. You have thirty to sixty minutes during the free appointment to get to know this person and to help them get to know you. During this time, you should be evaluating their strengths and weaknesses and using that information to show them how they need you. You have a captive audience. Consider it a soft sell, as they came to you for help. Bear in mind that while many people cannot afford a personal trainer weekly, many like to make appointments once a month to obtain a new program, monitor progress, and stay motivated. Be sure to offer this as an option if someone says that personal training does not fit into his budget.

 Alert

Word of mouth or referrals will be a great tool for developing and growing your client base. People feel more comfortable hiring someone with whom a friend or colleague already has a relationship. Do not be afraid to ask your clients if they feel comfortable giving you referrals.

If at the end of your initial consultation you have not sold a personal training package or session, make it easy for them to approach you in the future. Give them your business card, tell them you're available to address any questions or concerns, and that you hope you can work together in the future. If that person likes you and feels comfortable with you, they may refer a friend to you because you were professional and courteous.

Follow Up

Follow up is vastly important when you're selling anything. During a new member appointment, you can gather a great deal of information that will make following up easier and more effective. Most clubs have their members fill out a form or questionnaire during their first appointment. This form should at least include the member's name, phone number, e-mail address, occupation, fitness experiences, and hobbies and interests. There may be more information on the form, but these basics are all you need. From this information, you can develop a call list to generate personal training leads. You can make index cards, a computer list, or enter the information into a PDA. Send out an e-mail or handwritten note within a few days of your meeting. Tell the member you enjoyed meeting him or her and reiterate your offer to answer any questions that may arise. You may also choose to take this one step further and send out monthly e-mails with tips and information on areas of fitness such as weight training, nutrition, or stretching. This will keep you and your services at the front of people's minds and may help you acquire new clients.

Scheduling

One of the biggest challenges you'll face as a trainer is scheduling clients. The primetime hours are before and after work, and this is a finite amount of time. Most personal training takes place from 6–9 A.M. and 4–8 P.M., Monday through Friday. Depending on your particular place of employment, you may be scheduling your own clients, or the club may be doing it for you. Either way, it would be wise to work during either or both of these peak times.

Be cautious of new clients who want to work with you five days per week. Most clients begin with the best of intentions. They are motivated and positive, but don't realize what a big commitment they're making. If they lose their motivation and stop exercising as quickly as they started, you'll have five time slots to fill.

Discovering what your potential client does for a living is quite helpful in determining if and where they will fit into your schedule, and you into theirs. If they work a nine-to-five job, obviously they'll have less flexibility—they'll need to train either during peak hours or on the weekend. If they're self-employed, work from home, or are a stay-at-home parent, they may have more flexibility to train during off-peak hours. It is helpful to have clients with a variety of occupations, so you don't have a large gap in your schedule midday.

The most important factor in signing up a new client is whether they fit comfortably into your schedule. It isn't wise to rearrange your schedule for a new client who has not proven to be consistent and reliable.

The people who can afford to hire trainers multiple times per week are often business owners and executives and their spouses. These people are a great asset because they understand the importance of making and keeping appointments, as well as the value of your time. The drawback is that they tend to travel a great deal for business and vacations, which can leave you with several empty time slots if they are on the road for a week or more. Last minute cancellations can also occur due to unforeseen airline difficulties, extended business trips, and fatigue from traveling. This group of people will be your bread and butter and it is prudent to be flexible with them, within reason.

Drawbacks of Working in a Health Club

Health clubs are a great place to begin a personal training career. However, they're not always where the ambitious person wishes to remain for the long term. Many trainers will start at a club to gain experience and name recognition. Then they'll move on to open a studio or do independent training.

Job Hours

Most health clubs open around 5 A.M. and close around 10 P.M. They are open seven days per week and close only on major holidays. Depending on the location, some clubs, such as those in metropolitan areas, are open even longer hours. It isn't uncommon for trainers in these locations to work long hours, six to seven days per week. While this isn't a concern for the young trainer with endless energy and without a family, it's not typically a schedule that people can maintain for decades. On the other hand, small clubs generally don't have a great need for personal trainers, so there may be many low-paying desk hours and very little personal training. While the hours at small clubs are more manageable, it's difficult to make a good living in this situation. Of course, positions with the happy medium of reasonable schedules and a balance of personal training and desk hours do exist, but this is not typically the case in a health club setting.

 Fact

Clubs in larger cities need to cater to large populations of people working long hours. For this reason, clubs in these areas tend to have extended business hours and may even stay open twenty-four hours. If you work in one of these clubs, you may end up with the graveyard shift, especially if you're the new guy.

Working for Someone Else

When you work at a health club, you are not your own boss. You have to follow the rules and regulations that management sets for you. The club will, for the most part, set your schedule and rates. In addition, the club makes all of the policies for the personal training of clients, from the standard operating procedure for an initial consultation to penalties for cancellations. For some people, this is a positive, because it gives them structure. However, it may also limit your flexibility and creativity, which are aspects most personal trainers really enjoy about the profession.

Pressures

Some clubs require their trainers to sell a certain number of memberships, personal training packages, and/or nutritional products each month. Usually the larger, franchised clubs focus more on sales to increase revenue. There may even be a three to six month probation period for new trainers. During this probation time, management will monitor new trainers to see how they interact with members and other employees, as well as how successfully they make money for the club. While some people thrive in this environment, others may feel it causes unwanted stress and may choose to be in a less sales-oriented environment.

 ## Question

I feel like I have sales potential, but I don't have sales experience. Where would be a good place for someone like me to work?
As a personal trainer, you will have to sell to be successful. One way to strengthen your skills is through training and experience. Franchised health clubs such as Bally's Total Fitness are highly focused on sales. They will train you to sell and give you plenty of opportunities to practice doing so.

Another pressure of working in a club is competition from other personal trainers. There are a limited number of people who want and can afford a personal trainer. Since you will most likely not be the only trainer in your club, you are in direct competition with your colleagues for these members. That is why you must remain professional and personable at all times, and keep your knowledge and skills current. If you become apathetic, you may lose a potential client to a trainer who's more motivated than you. Even worse, you may lose a current client if you're not doing your job well. While competition can bring out the best in you and make you rise to the challenge, it may also increase job stress.

Compensation

There are several ways to be paid for your services at a health club. You may be on a set hourly rate, though this is rare. More typically, you'll have an hourly rate for working the desk and a different rate for personal training. The amounts vary greatly, depending on the location of the club and what the going rates are for personal training in that area.

The Split

While you make an hourly wage for running the fitness center, you usually work out a split for personal training. A split fee means that the club gets a percentage of the training fee and you get the rest. The split will vary from club to club; in some clubs it may be negotiable, in others it may be set. This is something to work out when you are hired. Typically, the split is 50 percent to the trainer and 50 percent to the club. As an entry-level personal trainer, your split may only be 40/60, but may become more favorable as you gain experience. Depending upon your experience and number of clients, you may be able to negotiate a 60/40 or even 70/30 split, but this is not typical. Keep in mind that the more clients you have, the more money the club will make and the more successful you'll be as a trainer.

Other Revenue Streams

There are other ways to make money in a health club. You may get certified to teach a group exercise class such as group cycling, kickboxing, aerobics, yoga, Pilates, or group weight training classes. These options add a nice variety to your workday, though they may not pay as well as personal training. Group personal training, however, does tend to be quite lucrative, and is also a good option for those who may not be able to afford one-on-one sessions.

Selling nutritional supplements is also a great way to add to your income. In some clubs, you can receive commission for selling weight loss/weight gain products. Use this outlet to your advantage, as you'll have people all around you looking for help to change their bodies. This is one tool you can give them to increase their chance for success.

Renting Space in a Health Club

Being an independent contractor at a health club is sometimes an option. This means that instead of being an employee of the club, you rent space from the club and conduct your own business within their facility. This is a good option if you're already established and have a good client base, or if you're really interested in being your own boss but can't afford to open a location on your own.

How It Works

Generally, when a trainer rents space at a club, he'll pay the club a set fee (rent) for the month. Depending on the size and location of the club, this may range from hundreds to thousands of dollars. A less common alternative is paying the club a percentage or flat rate for each client you train at the club. Club management and the trainer must figure out what is a reasonable arrangement for both parties.

The benefit of renting space is that you make your own schedule and come and go as you please. You don't have to sell or work for the club in any way. While you'll likely have to follow certain policies, you have a great deal more flexibility. You can train your clients the way you want to train, not the way designated by the club.

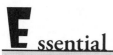

E ssential

If you're good at what you do, there is a very good potential income in this situation. You are making 100 percent of your hourly rate, and if you have good business practices, you can be very successful. You are limited only by the number of hours you can work.

The Risks of Renting Space

Because you're within a health club, you still have competition from other trainers. In fact, you actually have more competition, because management will try to steer potential personal training clients to the trainers that they employ. You don't have the benefit of meeting people during new member consultations because you won't be doing those types of appointments for the club. You also now have overhead costs because you're paying rent. This means that in order to make money, you have to make enough appointments to pay your overhead before you can make a profit. If you don't have enough clients, you'll actually lose money. Also, if you were an employee of the club, you'd be paid for the time you're there. However, as an independent trainer, you're not being paid for time between appointments.

Chapter 3

Corporate Fitness

Corporations are investing more money each year in the effort to help their employees stay healthy and fit. These corporations have learned that it is more economical for their business to help employees stay healthy than to pay the rising medical costs when they become ill. In order to ensure employees stay healthy, companies are frequently paying part of their employees' gym memberships or investing in some type of workplace fitness program.

What Is Corporate Fitness?

Corporate fitness is fitness facilities and wellness programs for the workplace. The programs may take place at that particular business, a nearby health club, or another facility. These programs increase job satisfaction and help keep employees healthy, especially since people are now working longer days.

As a trainer, working with people outside the four walls of your health club can be a great way to keep yourself motivated and energized, because you're changing your environment. Corporate fitness allows the trainer to experiment with different programming, and working with larger numbers of people can also increase hourly pay and overall salary.

There are several types of corporate fitness. The first type is the gym/fitness center in the workplace. The in-work fitness center is becoming increasingly common, but is also quite costly for companies to establish and maintain.

A less expensive, and therefore more common, alternative is for companies to partner with a nearby health club and work out some type of discount or reimbursement for its employees. This option has very little to do with personal trainers directly; it is an arrangement between the company and the health club. A third option is for a local health club or independent trainer to offer programming directly in the workplace on a certain time each day or week.

E ssential

Try to find someone within the company who can act as a liaison between you and the employees, preferably someone in upper management. This will help you learn what the employees want and need, and will make setting up programs much easier. You want to make the process as simple as possible, because time is money.

Training in the Workplace

The norm for most trainers is working one-on-one with clients. In a corporate setting, however, you most frequently work with groups of people. There are several factors you might consider while developing a corporate fitness program:

- How big is the area you will be utilizing?
- How many employees are in the facility?
- What type of company is it?
- Do they have their own equipment?
- Do you need to bring equipment?
- What type of training do you want to offer?
- When and how often will your program take place?
- What is the maximum number of employees you can handle at one time?
- Do you have the support of upper management?
- Who is going to pay for your services: the company, employees, or both?

Finding Companies to Work With

Landing corporate fitness accounts can be quite a challenge, as it requires the trainer to become a salesperson. First, you must research the companies in your area to see which ones might support this type of program. There should be at least 50 to 100 employees for the training to be worth your time. The more employees at a facility, the more likely it is that you'll have enough interest to run a successful program. There should also be a sizeable physical space to run the program. The company should have a room that is at least 400 square feet, though you can work with a smaller space if necessary. Once you find a company that fits the profile you're looking for, it's time to sell.

 Fact

You are more likely to land a corporate fitness account if you know or train someone who works for the company and can vouch for your skills, professionalism, and reliability. It's therefore wise to network with your personal training clients. Learn where they work and what they do, so you can see if your services might be needed in their place of business.

If you're going to be successful, you should have a good sales plan. First, decide how you'll make the initial contact with the company. Usually, the best way to make an initial contact is by mail. Be sure to include your resume/bio, services you can provide, a description of past and present corporate programs, and the features and benefits of using your services. These materials form your media packet, which will showcase your skills and experience for potential clients, and hopefully establish a relationship. This simple task can help you get in the door for a face-to-face appointment/presentation. You'll need to figure out who the contact person at the company should be (more on this below), send the letter to that person's attention, and then follow up with a phone call. Before you make any calls, write a script to work from, so you'll sound confident and professional and not forget any pertinent information.

Question

What is the difference between cold calls and warm calls?
A cold call is when you call on the phone or visit a company unannounced and try to sell your services. A warm call means the company is aware of who you are because you've made contact previously by mail, e-mail, referral, etc.

This follow-up call will hopefully bring about an appointment at the company for you to showcase your talents. Once you have your appointment set up, you must make a full sales presentation. It's important to adequately prepare and practice, as this isn't a task commonly performed by personal trainers. Be sure to have the following forms and information:

- Waiver and liability forms
- Health screening forms
- Proof of liability insurance
- Resume, if you did not already send it
- Program design including cost, dates, and times

It is important that you are as professional as possible. You should dress in business attire, be early for the appointment, and be prepared.

Finding the Right Contact Person

Determining who your contact person should be at each company is a very important task, and it may be as easy as getting referrals from your clients and other people you know. Talk to as many people as you can. Ask them about the company they work for: its size, location, and if they think there might be an interest in your services. If the answer is yes and the company meets your other requirements, find out from your referral source whom to contact.

If you're unable to get leads in your warm market (a market in which you have a networking partner), you'll need to do your own research and then contact the Human Resource Director or someone in a related position.

Try offering the company one or two complementary workouts to help generate interest and excitement in the employees. If management sees their employees' enthusiasm, they may be more willing to hire you. Remember, you're not going to close every sale. What might work at one company will not be a good fit for another.

E ssential

Networking is the name of the game. The more influential people you meet, the better your contact and referral system. Establishing strong business relationships is very important.

Benefits of Working in the Corporate Setting

Establishing corporate fitness programs will give you the opportunity to expand your personal training business. Working in a new environment is mentally refreshing, and also presents new networking opportunities. As a trainer, you should always be looking for potential clients. By offering these services, you'll be working with larger groups, increasing the number of people you come in contact with, and ultimately, your overall profitability.

A Change of Scenery

Changing the environment in which you work will help prevent you from becoming stale. While you may not be sitting behind a desk all day, working in a health club can start to feel redundant just like any other job. When you train at a new location, you're using different equipment and exercise protocols than you normally use. This can create excitement in you that will make your programs more exciting for your clients as well.

Potential Clients

Establishing yourself in a new environment can increase your client base. This is a great opportunity for a new pool of people to get to know you and your skills. These people may enjoy your group programs and want to train with you one-on-one, or they may refer you to someone they know. To maximize this opportunity, you need to do follow up. Hand out business cards and brochures to the participants in your programs. Make your corporate clients aware of any other services you offer, and make sure they feel comfortable contacting you with any questions or concerns.

 Alert

Handing out business cards or brochures about your services is crucial to attracting new clients. However, be careful not to come across as pushy or aggressive. Remember, you are in someone else's place of business to provide a service.

During your corporate training, you want to create the feeling that the company needs your services. Show the management team that you are a motivator, as well as a great source of health and wellness information. This will help ensure your longevity at the company. You also need to continue recruiting new employees into your program. There is always a certain dropout rate, so you'll continually need new people to ensure profitability. Periodically send out e-mails or newsletters with health information and invitations to join your program. You can also occasionally offer complementary workouts to pique interest in those who have not yet joined. You may even want to offer incentives for those already participating to recruit new employees. You could offer a free one-on-one training session to the person who recruits the most new people, or take half off the next series of classes. The incentive possibilities are endless.

Large Volumes/Training in Groups Increases Profit

Training people in groups has benefits for both the client and the trainer. For example, people tend to feel more comfortable in groups, and training becomes more social for everyone in attendance. Clients motivate, encourage, and support each other. In addition, because it's more affordable to train in a group, people who couldn't typically afford a personal trainer are able to benefit from your services.

E ssential

Training clients in groups increases your earning potential. You can train one person twice a week for $50 an hour and make $100. Or you can train twenty people who each pay $10 an hour twice a week and make $400. That's $2,000 in a five-week session versus $500 for doing a one-on-one for five weeks. You've quadrupled your hourly rate by increasing your hourly client volume.

Creating a welcoming, comfortable atmosphere can help generate more business. Developing one successful class or program within an organization may lead to the development of more programs within that same facility, or in other facilities within the company. If you create a successful program, the excitement will spread. Your best advertisement is word of mouth, and satisfied clients will tell their friends about you.

Expanding Your Business

As a trainer, you're only as successful as the hours in a day you're booked. If you are not training a client, then you are not making money. Even if you do have a schedule filled with clients, your income is limited by the number of hours in a day you're able to work. In order to make more money, you either need to increase your hourly rate or duplicate yourself. Subcontracting personal trainers out to businesses for your corporate fitness programs is one way to increase your earnings.

Programming

When providing corporate fitness services, it's best to offer a variety of exercise choices. You may offer one-on-one training, circuit weight training classes, conditioning classes, aerobics classes, yoga, Pilates, etc. The greater the variety, the more likely you are to appeal to a greater cross-section of employees.

Individual Personal Training

While it can be done, one-on-one appointments are not usually a great option for the corporate setting. You'll typically have three times during the day to train the corporate client: before work, after work, and at lunch. Therefore, individual appointments are not the best use of your time. The exception would be if someone could train during off-peak hours, which may be possible if someone has flexible time or can take their lunch later in the day. You'll also need to consider that not many people can afford this type of training, as it can run anywhere from $40 to upward of $100 an hour. You significantly decrease your pool of potential clients by offering only this type of training. However, if you leave it as one option, you may be able to do some one-on-one appointments.

Adult Conditioning Class

This type of program may consist of a combination of strength training and cardiovascular exercises, or it could also be a boot camp-style program. These classes are usually run by the session and have a certain start and end date. You may allow new employees to join at any time, but it's ideal for them to start with the first class, as the other participants will be more conditioned. By prorating for people who want to start mid-session, you establish good business relationships and help foster trust, which increases your overall volume.

Some key factors in developing and implementing this type of program are the frequency and duration of the program. People want to commit to getting healthy and fit, but their excitement and enthusiasm can wane over time. They also don't like to pay a lot of money at once. Usually, it's safe to start with a five- to six-week program, with a frequency of no more than two or three times per week.

Upon completion of the first session, you can evaluate its success and adjust these factors accordingly.

Surveys are great tools to help you evaluate the success of your programs. You won't know what people think unless you ask them, and you may receive some helpful feedback that you can implement in your next session. Some questions you might want to include in a survey are:

- Did you enjoy participating in this program? Why or why not?
- Will you participate in another session? Why or why not?
- Did you have fun?
- Did you feel the cost was fair and affordable? If not, why?
- Would you recommend this program to your coworkers? Why or why not?
- Did you achieve your goals?
- Is there anything that could be done to make this class better and more enjoyable?
- Comments or Questions?

Alert

Watch for participants who gradually stop attending class. Try to discover why they are no longer participating, and intervene if possible. Sometimes you will be able to help, and other times it will be out of your control.

The survey should be short and to the point. You may consider entering everyone who fills out a survey into a drawing for a free half-hour session with you. That will increase the number of responses you receive. Surveys help you expand on the good and eliminate the negative. Do your best to implement any reasonable changes that are suggested and correct problems as they are pointed out to you.

E ssential

Aerobic/Group Exercise Programs

The most important consideration with group exercise is certification. Many trainers are not certified to teach this type of program. If that's the case in your situation, then you'll need to subcontract a group exercise instructor.

Another important consideration is where within the company the program will take place. The room must be big enough to accommodate such a program, as well as having proper flooring. Safety is a primary concern, and a room that is too small or has concrete flooring could create an unsafe environment for exercise.

If you're subcontracting, you'll need to find reliable instructors. They are a reflection of you, so you want people who are professional and responsible. Canceling classes, tardiness, or no-shows cannot be tolerated. Obviously, situations will arise, but finding disciplined, dependable instructors will keep them to a minimum.

Drawbacks to Corporate Training

As with anything in life, there are certain drawbacks to dealing with corporate America. Budgets are always an issue with companies. Be aware that if the company is paying for your services and there are budget cuts, your programs will likely be cut back or eliminated. Your services are considered a privilege, not a necessity, and are therefore expendable. On the other hand, if the employees are paying for your services, then you're more insulated against budget cuts.

Preventing Boredom

Over time, people can lose interest in any workout program. Your job is to keep them interested and motivated. Developing new program ideas is essential to the success of your corporate fitness program. This is especially important if the company you're working with does not have its own fitness center. If you're using your own equipment and running specific programs throughout the day, then the company is depending on you. Constantly creating new programs requires a great deal of effort and can at times be frustrating. You must perform a balancing act of keeping it simple yet interesting.

Question

What is a group exercise instructor?
A group exercise instructor is an individual who is certified to teach classes such as aerobics, kickboxing, yoga, Pilates, etc. As with personal training, there are many certifying organizations, and it is important to have or hire someone with a reputable certification.

Interacting with Business People

Always remember that your clients in the corporate setting are at work. They may not feel as comfortable and relaxed as they might in a health club. If they're doing a lunchtime program, they may not want to sweat too much because they have to get back to work, so you have to consider this in your program design. You are also under time constraints because they will need to get back to work.

You are in a corporate setting, so behaving in a professional manner is of the utmost importance. Corporate rules and etiquette apply. Watch what you say and how you say it, always remembering where you are.

It May Not Last

Providing corporate fitness programs is a great way to expand your business and increase your overall income. However, the duration of these programs may at times be out of your control. The company paying for your services could be negatively impacted by the economy, and no longer able to afford to keep you. Management could change, and the new people may not want a corporate fitness program. There are many factors that may influence the longevity of your programs. Doing your research ahead of time may help decrease the risk of a failed program, but nothing is guaranteed.

Compensation

Your pay will be dictated by several factors. The first factor is whether you're just overseeing the corporate fitness center, or you're running your own programs. If you're simply running the fitness center, your hourly rate will be significantly lower than one-on-one or group training. If you're doing individual training, you should charge the same rate that you charge your other clients. However, you may consider offering half-hour sessions, as these are more feasible for people during work hours.

Group programs are where you can really increase your hourly rate. The exact amount will depend on how many participants you have, as well as whether the employees or the company are paying you. With ten or more people, you can keep the clients' costs down while increasing your own profit margin. Remember to consider the time it takes you to commute from your other place of business when you negotiate your fees.

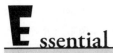

Be careful not to sacrifice service in an effort to increase profits. If you have more people than you can handle sign up for your programs, you will need to hire another trainer to assist you. It may decrease your profits initially, but it will increase satisfaction with the program and you will therefore be more successful.

Working for an Hourly Wage

If you're hired to run a corporate fitness center, you'll most likely receive $15–$20 per hour. Your job will be to create a safe and enjoyable atmosphere for the employees who exercise. As an employee of the company, you may or may not have the opportunity to offer personal training. If you do, it's still in your best interest to work with groups, as this will pay better than individual training. Working with four employees at a time who each pay $15 will give you $60. However, unless you're an independent contractor and can negotiate the opportunity to personal train, you probably won't be able to do so in a corporate setting.

Chapter 4

Personal Training Studios

Personal training studios are relatively new to the industry. They appeal to a more specialized market; mainly, clients who enjoy working in a private atmosphere with a personal trainer. Because virtually all of the people who workout in studios hire a trainer, there is substantial income to be made in this setting. There are many benefits to owning your own studio or working in one, such as financial freedom and being your own boss. Along with these benefits, however, come longer hours and greater responsibilities.

What Is a Personal Training Studio?

Personal training studios are smaller facilities that specialize in one-on-one and small-group training. Some studios also offer nutritional consulting, group exercise, massage therapy, and physical therapy. Many only allow their members to workout if they're with a trainer, and are open by appointment only. Members receive a great deal of individual attention, but at a considerable cost. There are significantly fewer studios in the fitness industry than there are health clubs and gyms, as they appeal to a very small portion of the population.

 Fact

Studios can be located virtually anywhere. Some trainers have studios set up in their home, garage, or office space. While many are small in size, they can be just as profitable as larger facilities.

Differences Between a Studio and a Health Club

Studios are quite different from health clubs. First, studios are typically much smaller, and therefore less costly, to run. Studios usually range from 300 to 3000 or more square feet, depending on the services provided there. Health clubs can be as large as 30,000–150,000 square feet, depending on the geographic location and surrounding population. Studios typically have between one and five trainers; a large health club may employ well over fifty people.

 Fact

According to IHRSA, personal training services account for the largest portion of revenue for both health clubs and studios.

Clients who exercise at a personal training studio enjoy the privacy and attention they receive. Some may feel embarrassed or intimidated at a health club, and are more comfortable in an environment with fewer people. Some clients may have special needs and find a studio less cumbersome to maneuver. They may also need a trainer to assist them in setting-up equipment and performing the exercises due to some physical limitations. However, health clubs tend to offer a greater variety of programs and services to their members. Unlike studios, that are limited by space and number of employees, health clubs have the means with which to offer programs that attract a more diverse group of people.

Personal training studios don't usually charge a monthly or yearly membership fee like health clubs do. These costs are built into the price of training sessions. They may, however, charge an initiation or application fee. Most sell personal training packages ranging from five to thirty or more sessions. The larger the package purchased, the greater the discount. By selling a large package, a trainer is ensured business over an extended period of time.

Quantity Versus Quality

Health clubs and gyms usually run on quantity. The more memberships sold, the larger the club's profit. This system works because a significant number of people who join a health club rarely or never use the facility. People sign up with the best of intentions, exercise for a few weeks, then stop going or only go sporadically. Their fees have already been paid, so the club does not lose money when people do this. In fact, they need people to be inconsistent, because if every person who signed up actually went and exercised, the facility would be very crowded.

 **Alert**

Be careful not to over or undercharge for your services. Find out how much other fitness facilities in your area are charging for personal training, and make sure you are comparable. You can and should charge more than a health club, because you are offering more customer service and attention. However, if there are other studios in the area, you should be in a similar price range.

Personal training studios, on the other hand, don't want or need to sign up large numbers of people. They need quality over quantity, meaning adequate numbers of dedicated clients who will consistently exercise with a personal trainer over long periods of time.

Daily Managerial Considerations

The studio setting is very different from a health club, where you have a support group to help you run the facility. Here you'll most likely begin by managing it alone. Since there is little or no income stream from memberships each month, the profit margins may be small at first. This can be balanced out, however, by the fact that overhead costs are lower.

If in the beginning you cannot afford to hire help, you'll have to work with clients and perform managerial duties simultaneously. But if this situation seems daunting to you, there are a few ways you can avoid it. If there is no money in your budget to pay for office and support staff, you have several options. You can charge your clients a nominal facility maintenance fee. This will immediately increase your monthly income.

E ssential

With the establishment of any new business, working long hours is normal. If this pace persists for an extended period of time, it could lead to burnout, and therefore reduced customer satisfaction. While working hard is essential, you must find a balance so that your personal and professional well-being are not put in jeopardy.

You may also consider renting space to other trainers. In this case, they will pay you a set fee each month and bring in their own clients. You may also allow trainers to subcontract, meaning for each appointment they have you are paid a percentage. These scenarios will obviously increase your revenue. This will also help you with your staffing issues, because you have more trainers around to answer phones and field questions from walk-ins. In addition, there will be fewer hours that you yourself must physically be there or that the business will be unattended.

If you do end up running the facility alone, you have several factors to consider and plan for:

- Who will answer the phone?
- What happens when a potential client enters while you are training?
- What happens if you become sick or injured?
- Will you allow your members to use the facility when they are not working out with you?
- Who will do the marketing and advertising?
- How many hours per day and week will you work?

These are all issues that you must work out ahead of time so they don't take your attention away from your clients. Your clients are paying a substantial fee for your undivided attention, and will not stay with you if you cannot provide it. The other major issue is that you don't want to lose potential sales because you are working with someone and can't answer the phone or door. The first impression is the most important for a potential client, and you need to have provisions in place for these scenarios.

If you choose not to have other trainers in the beginning or at all, you'll have to do some serious planning. First, you will need a smaller facility, because you alone cannot work enough to afford high overhead. Second, you'll need to have information ready for people who enter your facility looking to sign up. Set up a table with literature and a place for them to leave their contact information in case you are with a client. Finally, an answering service would be helpful, but voice mail will suffice if you don't want to pay the monthly fee. People do appreciate speaking to a person when they call a business, and answering services are a relatively inexpensive way to accomplish this.

 ## Question

How do I know what hours to remain open?
Check the hours kept by health clubs and other studios in the area to get an approximation of what your clients will expect. The other major issue is how many hours you and your staff can support. While you want to be open as much as possible, you don't want to burn out. This is a balancing act, and you may need some time for trial and error before reaching a final decision.

Hours of Operation

As discussed in earlier chapters, most people exercise around their work schedules. Many studios are open by appointment only. Studios are like any other fitness facility in that peak hours are before work, during lunch, and after work. If you're the only trainer, you could be working from 5–10 A.M., 11 A.M.–1 P.M., then again from 4–8 P.M.

Some studios remain open regardless of appointments. As this would be a fourteen- or fifteen-hour day for someone, this is typically only the case in a studio housing multiple trainers. Remaining open longer hours, even if it is by appointment only, allows the studio to compete with nearby health clubs and gyms. Hours of operation that are too limited will reduce profits and may deter potential clients.

The Process of Opening a Studio

Owning your own studio can be extremely rewarding and have many benefits if done properly. The start up and maintenance costs are significantly lower than opening a health club. Your initial investment would likely be between $10,000 and $100,000, versus close to a million dollars for a health club. However, as this is still a significant amount of money, failure could be financially devastating. Having a solid business plan will increase your chances of success. Creating a business plan will be discussed in detail in Chapter 10. In addition, you must be willing to commit to a great deal of hard work both before and after opening. You'll need to do extensive research and market analysis in order to find the proper location, which takes a good deal of time and effort. Finally, once you do open, you'll be working long days to get the business off the ground. Determination, dedication, and drive are a must if you want to be successful.

Ways to Fund Your Business

Initially, your primary consideration will be start-up costs. You must first figure out how much money you'll need to purchase equipment, lease a space, and pay your bills for the first six months. There are several common ways to obtain financing. You may choose to finance the project yourself. This may be accomplished using personal savings, refinancing or selling property, or using credit cards. The benefit is that you are in complete control of your business. All of the equipment belongs to you, and you are able to make all business-related decisions without answering to anyone. You also won't need to pay interest if you use personal savings. The downside is, that if you use credit cards, you may end up paying large interest rates, and if your business is not successful, you could find yourself in dire financial straits.

 **Alert**

> The use of credit cards to help finance your studio should only be considered as a last resort. Credit card companies charge high interest rates that make it more difficult to pay down your debt. If you do have to go this route, consider your interest part of your overhead when you do your budget.

Another option is procuring funds from friends and family. You may do this in exchange for equity in the company, interest on the loan, or simply loan repayment. The benefits to borrowing from people you know are that there is less red tape, and repayment is less costly and more flexible. However, you risk putting the people you care for in a difficult situation if your business fails. If you do go this route, you need to be sure they understand the risks so you don't run the risk of ruining your relationship or their financial security. It is also very important to have a business lawyer draw up a contract to make the agreement legal and protect your lender.

Private investors can be a favorable option if you can find them. These are typically established business people with some disposable income. If your business isn't successful, they may be able to write off their loss for tax purposes, and you won't personally lose a great deal of money. Before you choose this option, you must discuss with your investors what role they wish to play in your business. Will they simply mentor you, or do they want to have a say in the daily activities there? You must also decide on repayment. Some investors are only looking for a return on their investment, while others want to profit share. With the right investor, this can be a great situation for both parties. The main problem is in locating people willing and able to make this type of investment.

A significant amount of grants are available to small businesses. However, you must be amenable to doing the work to find and apply for them. Grants are an option for everyone, but are easier to obtain for women, minorities, veterans, and people catering to special interests. The Internet is a great resource in locating grant money. This endeavor is time-consuming and difficult, but can be well worth the effort, as you never have to repay the money.

If none of these options are available to you, you may consider applying for a loan from a small-business lender. This can be difficult, as small-business lenders typically loan money to businesses that have been in existence for at least two years. In addition, the process is long and the interest rates may be high. You'll need to provide a great deal of information, including: a written description of your business, personal financial statements, loan repayment plan, copy of your proposed lease, articles of incorporation, letters of reference, letters of intent, contracts, plans and specifications, and possibly more. You must also have collateral in the event you default on the loan. Lenders require the business owner to invest a certain amount (usually 15–25 percent) of their own money in the business. This demonstrates your belief in your undertaking. The personal risks of obtaining a small business loan are quite high. If you default, you can lose your collateral (your home perhaps), as well as ruin your credit.

Hiring Support Staff

A good support team is essential in running a successful business. You will require the services of an accountant in order to become incorporated. An accountant will also help you understand financial considerations such as taxes, budgeting, and planning your future. If you do choose to hire full-time staff, you'll also need to consider and understand payroll, workman's compensation, Social Security, and health benefits.

Hiring a business lawyer on an as-needed basis is also advisable. This person will examine your lease agreement, as well as any other contracts you may negotiate. You will have them as a resource if any issues arise with employees, taxes, insurance, lawsuits, etc. This is a key way to protect yourself and your business.

You will need to purchase many different types of insurance for your business, so it will be important for you to find a good insurance agent who specializes in small businesses. This person will help you determine what types of insurance you need, as well as how large your policies should be. You'll likely need liability and property insurance. You may also want to look into disability, health, and workman's compensation insurance. Insurance is not an area where you can afford to be lax. Do your homework and find a reliable, trustworthy, knowledgeable agent.

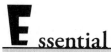
Essential

Some organizations that certify personal trainers also offer liability and health insurance to their members. There are also insurance companies that specialize in insuring health and fitness professionals.

Depending on the size of your facility, you may want to consider hiring maintenance and/or janitorial personnel. You won't have the time or energy to clean after working a ten- to fifteen-hour day. While you or the other trainers can pick up and do some light cleaning throughout the day, you'll need someone to sanitize the bathrooms and floors and wash down the equipment on a regular basis. You could hire a cleaning service or an individual. The most important thing is to make sure they are bonded and insured.

Working with Other Trainers

In the beginning, you may not be able to afford to hire trainers as your employees. If you do hire employees, you must know that there are laws governing insurance, Social Security, etc. for the people you employ that may make running your business complicated and expensive. An alternative is taking on independent contractors. The issue is finding trainers willing to work in your facility. These people must be skilled, professional, and trustworthy because your reputation is at stake. The good news is that if you're opening your own facility, you've probably been in the business for some time and know other trainers. There are also many online resources for finding trainers (see Appendix C). Just be sure to check their background, education, certifications, and references.

Costs of Operation

Operating costs will vary greatly depending on the size and location of your facility, as well as the services you offer. It would be impossible to give an actual figure, but there are some factors common to all businesses to consider. The first cost to consider is rent. This will be your biggest expense each month. There are also utilities, equipment maintenance, insurance, support staff fees, and taxes. Depending on how you funded your facility, you may also have loans or credit card debt to repay. Finally, you'll need to make enough money to pay your own personal bills. You must calculate these costs as accurately as possible ahead of time and have enough business to support your expenses before you open. It may take six months to reach the point where you're making a profit. It is critically important to prepare for this by borrowing or having enough money prior to opening.

Location, Location, Location

In order to be successful, your studio must be in a community that can afford and will utilize your services. You will need to do some research in order to make an educated decision. Examine the demographics of each community within a fifteen-minute driving radius from where you'd like to be located. Look at population, median household income, schools, and businesses in the area. If you already have an established clientele, you'll want to remain nearby so you don't lose them. People are too busy to drive long distances for a workout.

Once you decide on a city or town, you must find a space to rent or purchase. It is ideal to be in a place where people can see your business from the road and there is adequate parking. Other considerations are the locations of your competition. You don't want to open a place that's too close to another studio.

Equipment to Suit all Clients

There are many considerations when purchasing equipment for your studio. Obviously, space and budget are the biggest issues. Another issue is variety. You and your clients will be working in a relatively small space day in and day out. The last thing you want is for them to be bored or to be bored yourself. Functional training tools such as bands, medicine balls, and balance pads are a great and relatively inexpensive way to keep things fresh and interesting.

Other Professionals Employed by Studios

While personal training is the main source of income in a studio, there are many other services that can be offered as well, such as massage therapy, physical therapy, yoga, or Pilates. Studios that provide these services attract more clients, and are better able to satisfy the clients they already have. These services can also significantly increase revenue, but will be dependent upon the size of your facility. Keep in mind that you are running a studio, not a health club. You might consider one or two of these options, but trying to do all of them would force you to become a full-time manager.

Massage Therapists

Massage therapy and exercise complement each other well. It's a great service to offer your clients, and if you open it up to the public, it's also free advertising for your trainers. You simply need a private room that is no smaller than 8" × 10". It is also helpful if you can soundproof the room or put it near a quiet place. You can charge the massage therapist rent or work out a split the same way you would with a trainer.

Physical Therapists and Athletic Trainers

It is less common to have physical therapists (PTs) and athletic trainers (ATs) working in a studio. However, they too provide your clients with a great service. If a current training client becomes injured or has surgery, she can perform her rehab right in your facility. The reverse is also possible, where the clients who are released from treatment can be referred to one of your trainers for continued rehabilitation. Most of the equipment required by PTs and ATs will already be present in the studio. However, they will also need some additional space for treatment tables and therapeutic modalities.

Yoga and Pilates Instructors

You can utilize yoga and Pilates instructors in two ways. The first is to use them like trainers and have them do individual appointments. For this you'll need very little space. The second option is group classes. This may have a greater start-up cost, because you'll need a large room with the proper flooring.

Having these instructors in your facility is beneficial for your clients who need extra stretching and core strengthening. They also add variety and may attract different clientele to your business. Because of the increasing popularity of yoga and Pilates, these instructors should do quite well in a studio setting, and your clients will appreciate not having to travel to another facility for this type of workout.

E ssential

Whenever you employ or subcontract someone, your reputation is at stake. Be sure to perform thorough background checks on everyone you bring into your facility. Check their resumes for accuracy, call their references and previous places of employment, and also have their criminal background run. You want only quality, qualified people working in your establishment.

Other Instructors

A studio may benefit from employing other types of group exercise instructors if there is room for group classes. Members enjoy the variety of being able to do kickboxing and aerobics or take a dance class. You really do need a great deal of space for this, however, and that may be the deterring factor.

Obtaining and Keeping Clients

Because studios appeal to such a small market, it can be difficult to achieve and maintain a profitable client base. Marketing, advertising, and word-of-mouth referrals all play a role in obtaining new clients. You will likely spend a significant amount of time in the beginning marketing yourself and the studio. Successfully retaining clients will enable you to devote a smaller amount of time networking and advertising, and more time actually training. Keep in mind, however, that there will always be a need for new clients, because people will stop or take breaks from exercising. Therefore, even if you feel your schedule is full, you should spend about 20 percent of your time trying to increase your client base.

Alert

You need to continuously take on new clients, as you never know when you'll lose a client. People you work with may lose their motivation or become unable to train. If you become complacent and rely solely on the clients you have already, you may find your income dwindling.

Types of Clientele

People who will pay the premium for working out in a studio do so because they enjoy the privacy and special treatment they receive. A small portion may also require individual attention due to special physical needs. Due to the significant financial commitment, most of your clientele will be quite well-off financially. They are typically business owners, self-employed, business executives, investors, etc. There are also people who make modest incomes but sacrifice and save in order to be able to afford this service. It is important not to pre-judge potential clients. If someone is interested in buying a package, sell it to him. You never really know what people's financial situations are like. Your bread and butter clients, however, will tend to be those who are financially sound. They can afford to train for extended periods of time, and if the economy slows, they're insulated enough that it won't deter them from continuing to train.

Where Do I Find My Next Client?

Potential clients are all around you. Every person you encounter may be a future client, so always be prepared to market yourself. Even when you are out of the studio, you should have brochures and business cards with your contact information on hand. Strike up conversations with people wherever you go. While they may not need or be able to afford your services, they may know someone who does need them and can afford you. You are your own best advertisement, so be professional and courteous at all times.

You will also need to do some actual advertising. Some will be free and some will require a small investment. You can begin by creating flyers to hang in public places such as libraries or supermarkets. You may also ask local businesses such as restaurants you frequent if you can post your information. Many times nail, tanning, and hair salons will allow you to put out information, especially if you personally give them business. In turn, you can put their business information in your facility.

E ssential

Establishing a rapport and referral network with local physicians, podiatrists, chiropractors, physical therapists, and massage therapists is an invaluable tool for obtaining clients. They can provide an endless stream of new people. It is also nice to have trusted professionals to refer your existing clients to when necessary.

You may need to periodically place an ad in a local newspaper or magazine. You could also send out a mailing or leave pamphlets door-to-door. These options are more costly, but can generate interest in and knowledge of your services with the surrounding community.

Promotions

Promotions are a great way to attract new clients. There are numerous ways to go about doing this. You can offer your current members a free session for referring someone who purchases a package. You could also offer a free half-hour session to the first twenty people who come in for a tour of the facility. You could give a free nutritional consultation or $50 worth of supplements to any new member who purchases ten or more sessions. Offering specials around major holidays and the New Year is a great way to sell gift certificates and pre-sell training packages. The possibilities are endless. You simply need to be creative. Remember that while people love feeling like they're getting something free, be sure that you are not giving too much away.

 **Alert**

Remember that your clients in a studio spend a great deal of money every month to work with you. You can make them feel special and appreciated by offering a free or reduced session for their birthday. This type of promotion and service goes a long way toward keeping a client long term.

Working at an Established Studio

If you are not in a position to open a studio, you may choose to work in one. If you go this route, it would be wise to have at least a few clients before you start. You could also work part time at the studio and part time in another setting to supplement your income until you're established. Working in a studio allows you to hone your skills as a trainer and focus intently on your clients, because you have fewer miscellaneous tasks to perform in a studio than in a health club.

Benefits of Working at a Studio

There is a higher demand for your services at a studio than in a health club because everyone who goes to the studio must work with a trainer. If you're going into a studio that has been in business for some time, chances are the owner will have clients already there for you to pick up. They are probably already advertising, so new people should be joining regularly, and in very little time you should have enough clients to make a nice income.

Negotiating Payment

It is unlikely that you will be on a salary as a trainer in a studio. Typically, you will either be paying rent or doing some type of percentage split with the owner. You will have to negotiate how much rent you are paying or what percentage of your profits you will give up. You may be able to work out a deal where you pay a reduced amount for the first three to six months until you're established.

Ways to Increase Your Income

You might consider selling nutritional supplements if the studio does not promote its own line of products. This is a good way to make some extra money. You need to do some research and find a product line you feel comfortable promoting. You can also do things outside of the studio such as outdoor conditioning programs, in-home personal training, or even corporate fitness. If you can be creative and have vision, you can generate many opportunities to increase your income.

If you will be splitting the hourly session rate, try negotiating a sliding scale with the owner. Your first twenty clients might be a 50/50 split, clients twenty-one to thirty a 55/45 split, and over thirty a 60/40 split.

Making Your Schedule

You need to determine what hours and days you are willing to work. Until you have enough clients to support yourself, you won't have much choice when you'll work; you'll have to work when you can get appointments. However, one can only work so many late nights, early mornings, and weekends without burning out. Even in the beginning, put some limits on what your hours will be. For example, some people will not work Sunday, but will work Monday through Saturday. Some will work every other weekend or five days and three nights. Whatever your lifestyle is like, be sure you set boundaries so you can maintain your sanity and job satisfaction.

Chapter 5

Independent Training

Independent training may be broadly defined as being self-employed. However, while all independent trainers basically own and run small businesses, each of these businesses is unique. Independent trainers are entrepreneurs; they work in a variety of settings performing a multitude of programs and services. Therefore, providing a specific definition of independent training is difficult. Despite this, the following should provide you with enough information to help you decide whether or not this is a desirable and feasible means of employment for you now or in the future.

Benefits of Independent Training

There are many advantages to being an independent trainer, and countless reasons why people choose to be self-employed. The self-employed have a great deal of freedom and flexibility, as well as tremendous potential for success. People who work for themselves tend to feel happier and more fulfilled than those who are employed by others. You also have an opportunity to make more money.

Being In Charge of Your Own Destiny

The biggest benefit to independent training is being your own boss. When you work for others, they make most of the decisions on issues such as hours, scheduling, rates, salary, and benefits. When you are on your own, you decide when you will work, who you will work with, and how you will develop and implement your programs. You are the one who sets and enforces all policies. For the self-motivated individual, this is a thrilling and rewarding prospect. With few exceptions, the harder you work, the more fruitful the outcome.

 Fact

The Bureau of Labor Statistics found that 10 percent of all U.S. workers (approximately 10 million people) are self-employed. Considering there are approximately 290 million people living in America, that's less than 3.5 percent of the population. Working for yourself can be gratifying, but it also takes a great deal of discipline to be successful.

Enjoying Variety and Flexibility

As an independent contractor, you have unlimited options for when and where you'll work. You're not stuck in the same environment all day. Each day you will be working with different people in different places at different times. If you enjoy stability, this option is obviously not for you, but for the adventurous person, it is ideal.

Significant Tax Benefits

Being self-employed brings many tax benefits. You will pay lower income tax due to the numerous write-offs. For example, if you have a home office, which you should, you can write-off a percentage of your mortgage interest, property tax, and utilities. You can also write-off office supplies, Internet service, business or cell phones, and automotive expenses, among other things. In order to maximize your deductions and address your specific needs, you'll need to work with a C.P.A.

According to the *Wall Street Journal,* independent contractors are paid an average of 20–40 percent more per hour than employees performing the same work. Keep in mind, however, that independent contractors are only paid for the services they provide and do not receive vacation time, retirement, or medical benefits. Therefore, the extra money must be put toward planning for these circumstances.

In-Home Training

Clients who prefer to exercise in their homes do so for a variety of reasons. They may feel uncomfortable in, or simply not have time to go to, a health club. Whatever the reason, these people want a trainer to come to them. If you can find ten to fifteen clients who will workout with you multiple times per week and who live relatively close to each other, this can be a great full-time income. If that is not possible in the beginning, you can supplement your income by working in another setting such as a health club.

Why Offer In-Home Training?

There are several advantages to in-home training. First, your clients will cancel their appointments less frequently than in other settings. They will also almost never be late or not show up, because the appointment is in their home and they are already there. People who train in-home tend to be more flexible with when they can workout because they generally either own or run a business, work from home, don't work, or work only part time. You can also charge more for these appointments, as they take up more of your time due to commuting.

Essential

Although your home clients may not be late for an appointment, you may have to deal with more intrusions that take away from training time. The phone may ring, young children may interrupt, or someone may come to the door. Interruptions are a part of the experience when training someone in their home.

Equipment Considerations

With in-home training, you can expect your clients to have or purchase a certain amount of equipment. Some will have home gyms already, some will ask you to set up their home gyms, and others will wish to purchase as little equipment as possible. Available space and budget will be the two main considerations in purchasing equipment. Keep in mind that many everyday objects in the home can also be utilized during your workout. For example, coffee tables or couches may be used for benches. Stairs are also a great way to incorporate cardiovascular intervals, you could use the bottom stair in lieu of an aerobic step. Transporting equipment in and out of your clients' homes can be time-consuming and cumbersome, so whatever you bring needs to be small and versatile. Don't go overboard when purchasing equipment to bring with you. You may even be able to buy some things then sell them to your clients for them to keep. By doing this, you can increase your profit and minimize what you must transport.

You may purchase equipment on the Internet, from fitness equipment stores, or in sporting goods stores. Shop around to find the best prices and quality. Equipment from sporting goods stores is often not the best quality, and will not last long with daily use. The exception to this is dumbbells, which are pretty much the same everywhere. Fitness equipment companies that specialize in home sales will provide the best product for the price. Appendix B contains a list of reputable companies who sell exercise equipment.

In order to provide a good workout, your clients should at least have dumbbells, a stability ball, and a medicine ball. The weights will vary depending on their ability level. Exercise bands and rubber tubing are a nice substitute for dumbbells. They fold up, are easy to carry, and you can adjust the resistance to fit your clients' needs. Medicine balls, which come in a variety of weights and sizes, are another versatile piece of equipment that's portable and relatively inexpensive. Stability balls can be used in place of weight benches, abdominal machines, and squat racks. Balance pads and discs are nice to use with your better-conditioned clients to add a challenge to their workouts. While it is not necessary to purchase all of these types of equipment, they can help you keep your clients interested and your workouts fresh and exciting without putting a kink in your budget or theirs. When it comes to using home equipment, you're limited only by your imagination.

Here is an example of the potential cost of home equipment you may purchase:

Sample Equipment Costs from Perform Better		
Product	Quantity	Cost
Eight-Pound Medicine Ball	1	$39.95
Twelve-Pound Medicine Ball	1	$49.95
Economy Exercise Mat	1	$34.95
JC All-Purpose Exercise Bands Low Resistance	1	$24.95
JC Heavy-Resistance Band	1	$24.95
55cm Stability Ball	1	$26.95
Airex Balance Pad	1	$49.95
Total Excluding Tax and Shipping		**$251.65**

Drawbacks to In-Home Training

There is a significant amount of commuting involved in training in the home. This will take up large blocks of time, especially if you are driving in heavy traffic. You may miss or be late for appointments due to accidents, construction, etc., and if you are late for one appointment, it can throw off your schedule for the entire day. You will use a lot of gas and place a good deal of wear and tear on your vehicle as well. You will need to take these facts into consideration when setting your rates and scheduling your appointments.

 Question

What should I do if I am late for an appointment?
If you are running late, call your client and make them aware of the situation as soon as possible. You can offer to either discount the session, or if schedules permit, you may extend the appointment into the next hour. If the client prefers, simply reschedule. As long as this is an infrequent occurrence, no further action is necessary.

Another drawback to in-home training is the size of the space you are using. Most likely, you'll be working in a relatively small area with limited equipment. Because of this, you'll have to really use your imagination and creativity to prevent boredom for both yourself and your client.

Outdoor Training

Outdoor training is simply personal training outside. It is typically done in groups, either large or small. However, some individual clients enjoy exercising in this setting at least some of the time, as it adds variety to their training. The actual programming can be whatever you want it to be. If you enjoy working with athletes, you can organize sport-specific outdoor training where the programs work to increase certain athletic skills such as foot speed and agility. There is also a significant market for adult conditioning (often referred to as boot camps), where the program is designed to help get the average person stronger and into better cardiovascular conditioning. Whatever your vision, outdoor training can add diversity to your schedule, and because you're training in groups, it's also quite profitable.

Finding a Location

Finding a place to hold your programs should not be too difficult. You might consider a public school track or a park with an open field. These settings are typically free to the public, but you'll need to check with the local Parks and Recreation Department to be certain. It's helpful, but not essential, to have a track to use, because the distance is premeasured and the surface is ideal for running.

What Equipment Will You Need?

The equipment you will need will vary slightly depending upon the programs you implement, as well as on your budget. There are two main factors to consider when purchasing equipment. First, is the equipment easily transportable? Chances are you'll be traveling to your location and will need to keep the equipment in your car. You should be able to fit it easily in your car and be able to carry it to and from your vehicle. Second, is the equipment cost-effective? In order to be cost-effective, equipment should have multiple uses and be easily adaptable to different ages and abilities. Medicine balls, stability balls, and exercise bands are several items that fit these criteria.

Planning for Inclement Weather

When you create outdoor conditioning programs, there is always the issue of bad weather. Ideally, you should have a place to take people if this does occur. You may be able to rent a gym at a local Boys and Girls Club or YMCA. You may also be able to rent a group exercise room at a local health club. If you are creative, you should be able to find a space within a five to ten minute drive from wherever your program is typically held. If this is not a possibility, be sure to plan for rain dates.

 Fact

Training outside offers a great opportunity to advertise and promote your business, because you are highly visible while conducting a program outside. You can display a professionally made banner with your company name and contact information next to where you're training. That way people who see what you're doing can call or e-mail you for more information.

Renting Space in Other Businesses

You may be able to find a health club, studio, country club, physical therapy clinic, or other business that is willing to have you train in its facility independently. This can be a win-win situation for both you and the company you rent from. As a trainer, you'll be generating money for the club because people who want to train with you will sign up as members. It is also a great way for you to supplement your income, as well as get your name out there and network with other trainers and potential clients.

Benefits and Risks

There are several benefits to renting space in an established business. For one, the equipment is already there, so you and your clients won't need to invest in any. In addition, you won't have to spend as much time commuting, so you can schedule more appointments in a day. This may allow you to keep your per-hour rates lower and more affordable for people. Finally, because you are training in a place where other people can see you, it is like having free advertising for your services, and it makes it easier to obtain new clients.

E ssential

If your advertising options are limited, the best way to promote yourself is word of mouth. The club may not allow you to use print ads, so you need to work with your present clientele and ask for referrals. People value the advice of their friends, so your clients' recommendations of your services should help generate new business.

You need to consider that many health clubs and gyms do not want or allow independent trainers, because they are in direct competition with the trainers employed by the club. If you are permitted to train independently, you will most likely be required to sign a contract outlining the terms of your agreement. Unfortunately, this contract does not guarantee that you will be able to train at this facility for the long term. Another risk to renting space is that your overhead may be greater than your income if you don't have enough clients. Therefore, you will need to figure out if the cost of renting is worth it for you.

What Are Your Limitations?

Advertising can be a limiting factor when renting space in a health club. Find out if the club will allow you to advertise your services and what the restrictions will be, if any. Can you put up flyers? Can you hand out brochures and business cards? Can you offer free lectures to increase your warm market? The more visible you can be, the more business you will generate. If the club does not allow this type of advertising, your potential for growth will be stunted.

Pricing can limit your business in a club. Before you decide to work in a club and set your rates, you will need to find out what the other trainers at the club are charging. There are a couple of different ways you can set your prices. If you don't have many clients or much experience, you could price yourself slightly lower than the other trainers. If you are too low, however, people will not see your service as valuable. You may also set your rates to be equivalent to the other trainers, which is wise if your experience is equal to theirs. Finally, if you have significantly more education and/or experience, you can set a slightly higher rate. You will need to be able to justify this and the rate should not be dramatically different, or you will price yourself right out of business.

Alert

Before you decide to rent space from a club, survey your in-home clients and evaluate their level of interest in following you. It may be that you will lose all or most of your current clientele, in which case you may want to reconsider you decision. At the very least, you will know what to expect if and when you make the move.

If you already have an existing in-home training business, then the location of the health club can be a limiting factor. If your clients are already accustomed to training at home, having them switch to a club may be a difficult sell. If you choose to do this, the gym should be located no more than fifteen minutes driving time from the majority of your clients to make it as accessible as possible. Time is precious to people, so the more time it takes them to get to you, the less likely they will be to come. When switching from in-home training to renting space, you may lose 10–20 percent of your existing clientele. Losing two or three clients who train multiple times per week could mean having to fill five or more sessions per week. This is no easy task. You might consider continuing to travel to a few clients' homes until you build a new client base at the club.

Contract Negotiations

When you rent space in another business, you must cover your rent before you can make a profit. It is therefore in your best interests to negotiate the lowest rent you can. If possible, try to get the first three to six months rent at a discount so you can build your clientele. After the initial time period has passed, you should have enough business to pay your full rent and make a sufficient profit.

E ssential

Another option that might be better for a trainer who is just beginning, is to pay the club either a percentage of each session you perform or a flat rate for each person you train. For example, you might negotiate to pay the club 20 percent or $10 for each client you train. If you train ten people a week (forty people per month) at $50 per hour, you will make $2,000 and pay the club $400 from that. That is a profit of $1,600 for the month. If you were paying a set rent of $800, you would only make $1,200. On the other hand, if you train thirty people in a week at that same rate, you would make $6,000 and pay the club $1,200 from that. You are taking home $4,800, but if you paid the set rent, you would only have paid $800. This example demonstrates that when you are starting out, it may be better to pay a percentage or set rate on each client. That way, if it takes some time to build your client base, you are not sweating huge overhead. The problem with this is that when you do have a significant number of clients, you could end up paying more on a per-client basis than you would have for a set amount of rent. One way to avoid this problem is to try to negotiate a cap on the amount you will have to pay the club if you are paying per client.

Another way to negotiate rent is to offer to perform various services in exchange for training at the facility. You may give free lectures to groups of members or perform a certain number of new member consultations per month at no charge. By doing this, you may be able to train there for reduced or free rent. This is also a great way to meet people and add to your client base.

Another factor you will need to settle in the contract is advertising. You should put in specific terms how you are allowed to advertise and network. Will you be allowed to place flyers and brochures in the club? If so, will you have to pay to do so or is it included in your rental fee? Can you offer trial sessions and give seminars? Covering all of your bases will ensure a smooth transition and will help you know exactly what to expect. These issues are important, because advertising and networking are crucial to the growth of your business, and you do not want to find out once you are there that you are restricted in these areas.

Drawbacks to Independent Training

While being your own boss has many benefits and can be both rewarding and gratifying, there are also some downsides. It can be more difficult and more costly to find new clients. Because you are working for yourself, you need to continually promote yourself and your business. You need to be thinking two steps ahead, always networking for your next client. Your job security is you and how hard you work; there is no time to rest on your laurels.

It May Be More Difficult to Obtain New Clients

When you work for a health club or gym, you interact with a large volume of people on a daily basis. This allows you to do a great deal of networking for your new clients. Your warm market is quite large. When you work independently, you interact with far fewer people and therefore your warm market is significantly smaller. Because of this, you will have a greater reliance on referrals from your current clients.

Lack of Employee Benefits

When you are a full-time employee at a business, you receive vacation time, health benefits, sick days, and retirement benefits. When you work independently, you must provide these benefits to yourself. This requires a great deal of planning, as well as money. If you do not have a spouse with health benefits, you will need to find a company from whom you can purchase insurance. If you do this through your local small business association or chamber of commerce, it is still costly, but will be a reduced rate. Price out the type of plan you want and need, and budget accordingly. You can bank vacation time and sick days by putting money into a separate account, so you can afford to pay your bills even when you take time off of work. Finally, you will want to open a Roth IRA or some form of retirement fund, and pay into it each month so you are not forced to work until you are eighty. A financial advisor can help you plan where and how much to invest based on your individual needs.

How to Be Successful

What constitutes success as a personal trainer? How is it measured? Is it the amount of money you make, how many clients you have, how long you have been in business? You might say, all of the above. There are many factors predictive of success. You must have a strong work ethic to get started and be successful. The proper education, a dynamic personality, and determination are the keys to get you moving toward success. Keep in mind that people do not typically begin their careers as independent trainers, though it can be done. Most trainers start by working in an already established business and choose to go out on their own once they have gained experience, reputation, and a solid clientele.

Building and Maintaining a Client Base

In order to be a successful personal trainer, you must develop an extensive client base. Doing so will require significant time and energy. It may take up to six months or longer to obtain enough clients so you are working twenty to thirty hours per week. Your current location and the type of community you work in will influence the ease with which you grow your business. The more affluent the community, the easier it can be to grow. Because personal training is considered a luxury by many, be sure to focus your marketing on people who need and can afford your services.

Once you have established your core clients, you will still need to spend time maintaining. There is usually a group of clients who remain with you for extended periods of time, and others who come and go. There will always be a need to replenish those who do not reschedule or are inconsistent. It is also nice to have a cushion, so when things slow down you can fill empty time slots. A successful trainer is never complacent about finding new clientele.

E ssential

Because you will have less face-to-face contact with potential clientele as an independent trainer, you may find yourself tempted to spend more money on advertising. This may not be in your best interest, as it decreases your profit margin. Networking is the least-expensive way to obtain new clients, and should be your primary focus.

Preparing for the Slow Times

As with any business, there will be busy, profitable periods cycling with slower, less profitable times. This will typically depend on the time of year, but cannot always be predicted. Slow times tend to be around the holidays and school vacations. Being aware of this can help you be prepared so you do not suffer financially. If you know a client will be going on vacation, you can do a couple of different things. First, you can suggest to the client that they schedule extra sessions with you before they leave, as everyone likes to look their best when they are away. You should consider trying to schedule your own vacations during the times you know you will be slow, so you lose a minimum number of appointments. You can also try to find other clients to fill in the gaps while your regulars are away. Finally, you will need to put money away during your busy times so you have a financial cushion when business is slow or when you wish to take time off.

Creating Passive Income

Passive income is money you receive regularly without having to perform additional work. You may have to work for it to begin with, but once the system is in place, there is little or no more effort on your part. When you have a passive income, you receive money even when you do not work. This is beneficial because when you are self-employed, you do not have an employer who will pay you for your vacation and sick time. You would therefore have to tap into your savings during the times you take off of work. Passive income makes this unnecessary, or at least decreases the amount you need to take from your savings. When you are working and you have passive income in addition to your regular pay, you are increasing your profits. This money can be used to plan for retirement, reinvest in your business, or to create even more passive income. Think of it as insurance.

The most obvious way to create passive income is to hire another trainer to work for you. Once you have a full schedule, you can take on another trainer or even more than one, and have them pay you rent or a percentage of their hourly rate. If your trainers make $50 per hour and you receive 20 percent, you are making an additional $10 per hour, per trainer. With only one trainer performing twenty sessions per week, you will earn an extra $400 per week. If you can increase that to two or three trainers, you will earn an extra $800–$1,200 per week without increasing the amount of time you are working.

Chapter 6
Sports-Performance Training

Sports-performance training, also called sport-specific training, is a fun and exciting approach to expand your client base and increase your revenue. If you choose to do this type of training, you will most likely be working with recreational, school-age, or college-level athletes. The goal is to help them become better athletes through intense physical training. The beauty of sports-performance training is that it can be performed anywhere, and with very little equipment. The programs you run and settings you work in will vary depending upon the age and ability of your clientele.

Evolution of Sports-Performance Training

Sports-performance training is rapidly increasing in popularity. As little as ten years ago, only college or professional athletes had strength and conditioning coaches, whereas now many high schools employ strength coaches and trainers. Young student-athletes today are participating more in organized sports, while in the past, they played neighborhood pickup games. They are also specializing more in one sport. Instead of playing three or more sports, kids are choosing to play one or two and playing them year-round. The results are an increase in the levels of skill and competitiveness, as well as injuries and muscular imbalances.

Why Is this Training Unique?

Sports-performance training is unique because you are trying to improve very specific skills. When you perform traditional personal training, your general goals are to increase overall strength and cardiovascular conditioning. When you train athletes, you will be working to improve foot speed, agility, vertical-jump height, and power to name a few. Your entire program revolves around the athletic season and the specific skills required for the athletes' sports and positions. This is a much more complicated type of training, but is also quite fun and interesting for trainers who enjoy athletics.

 Fact

Athletes need to perform under great physical and emotional stress. Game situations involve a tremendous amount of pressure, and training should mimic competition as closely as possible. Therefore, the level of intensity is a huge factor when working with athletes. The more advanced your athlete, the higher the physical and mental intensity of the workout.

Selling Your Services

Selling your services to an athlete is easy. All competitive athletes want to reach their full potential and be the best they can be. The issue is that most of the time the athlete is not the person paying your fee; it is the parents, coaches, or school. If you try to sell yourself to the athletes, you are wasting your time. You need to present the benefits of your services directly to the decision-makers. Since the person paying for the services will not see an immediate return on investment, you will have a tough sell. Consider selling your services on the fact that the athletes will gain:

- Strength
- Muscular endurance
- Power
- Injury prevention
- Speed
- Agility and balance

Emphasizing these benefits to a potential client during a presentation can help increase your potential sales. You must overcome the price objections: "it's too expensive" or "it's not cost-effective." You can accomplish this by stressing the skills the athletes will improve by performing sports-specific training. Remember, most athletes want to be better, and most parents will bend over backward to help their children reach their goals. If you are still finding price to be a major objection, you can create small group sessions to make your services more cost-effective.

E ssential

Working with adolescents requires different skills and strategies than working with adults. Having an understanding of this age group and prior experience working with student athletes will increase your chances of success. Demonstrating a positive attitude and exhibiting empathy will help you gain their trust and respect. If they respect you, they will listen to what you say.

Interacting with Young People and Adults

There are many differences to consider when dealing with adolescent versus adult athletes. Your approach will vary significantly with the age of your clientele. Emotionally, adult athletes tend to be more mature, disciplined, and motivated. In addition, adults are physically more mature and developed, where adolescents are still in the process of growing. The musculoskeletal systems of adolescents are not fully developed, which demands extra attention when you are creating your programs. The adult athlete can handle a much more physically demanding workout. Adolescents will tend to have less strength and endurance, so your programs for this group will not be as advanced, but they should find it no less challenging.

When you choose to work with adolescents, you should be very structured and specific with your expectations. Their immaturity necessitates rules be in place in order to keep them focused and in line. You will not want to spend the short time you have disciplining your athletes. So make it clear from the beginning that you will not tolerate disruptions. You want their experience to be enjoyable, but chaos does not lend itself to a good working environment.

Another consideration when working with adolescents is their motivation. You should have a feel for where each athlete's motivation is coming from. Is she in your program willingly in order to become a better athlete, or did her parents or coach persuade or force her to join? The athlete's motivation will determine how willing she is to participate and how hard she's willing to work. Understanding the student's motivation will help you know how to coach her.

Working with adolescents can be a juggling act. There are many considerations and factors that must be taken into account when creating and implementing programs. The key is becoming educated on this age group and the issues that may arise. Being prepared can help ensure a smoothly run program, and will ultimately make your programs more profitable.

Income Potential and Financial Considerations

Your income potential will depend mainly on the setting you work in. A strength coach employed by a college will have different salary and benefits than one employed by a high school. Your work hours and ability to make money on the side will also be quite different. It can actually be more lucrative to work full time in a high school than at a college, depending on the NCAA division. You will also work fewer overall days in a high school, because most college positions are twelve months long.

If you are a self-employed sports-performance trainer, your income will be even more variable. It will depend on how many programs you run, how many people are in each program, and how much you charge for your services. Because most sports-performance training is done in groups, it can be quite profitable if you are self-employed. A group of ten athletes who each pay $15 per session will provide you with $150 per session. That is a nice rate. Keep in mind that you will likely have to reinvest some of that money into advertising and purchasing equipment. You will also not be receiving benefits or vacation time as you would if you were employed at a school or university, which may be a factor to consider.

Youth Fitness and Training Programs

Two main issues have prompted a dramatic increase in the demand for training young children. The first is a significant increase in childhood obesity. Because obesity in children is now considered an epidemic in the United States, there is a growing focus on increasing physical activity. Despite this issue, there has been a decrease in physical education classes in schools across the country due to budget concerns. Some school departments are also cutting sports from the budget in an effort to decrease spending. Youth fitness programs are one significant way parents can keep their kids active and healthy. The second factor increasing demand for youth training is the younger ages at which kids are beginning to play organized sports. Competition is more intense and people are looking for ways to give their kids an advantage. With the additional skills and conditioning, their child may make a team or get more playing time than someone who did not participate in a training program.

 Fact

In 1994, one in five children was overweight. By 2004, only ten years later, one in three children were found to be overweight. As a result, the incidence of Type II diabetes among children has skyrocketed, and nearly 50 percent of all newly diagnosed cases of diabetes are Type II.

How to Begin Training Children

The first step to beginning a program is deciding what population you wish to focus on. If you want to work with athletes, you could create after-school programs, summer youth programs, or sports clinics. If you are more interested in health issues, you may choose to create programs for overweight children, sedentary children, or children with a specific illness such as Type II diabetes.

Once you have narrowed your focus and have your ideas on paper, you can begin networking. You need to connect with adults who are influential with young people and their parents. The parents are the decision-makers and are paying for your services, so you have to convince them of the worth of the program. Coaches, teachers, administrators at local Boys and Girls Clubs or YMCAs, and pediatricians already have rapport with large numbers of parents. If you have relationships with anyone in those types of positions, contact them about what you are trying to accomplish and see if they will help you spread the word.

Alert

A key to successful selling is following up. Send periodic reminders to the decision maker by e-mail, postal mail, or a phone call. If it is cost effective, you can send a brochure or flyer containing pertinent information about your programs.

If you wish to create programs for overweight children, you will need to advertise somehow. You might think about networking with the local PTA or school committee to do some joint programs with them. You could also contact the local children's hospital and/or pediatricians in the area. They are good starting points because they can refer children with health-related weight concerns to you. Start by sending a cover letter with a brief description of who you are and what you would like to do. Be sure to include your resume and references. Follow up with a phone call so you can discuss what programs they have in place already, and what they feel the need is for your services. Many children's hospitals have dietary programs but not movement programs, because they lack the space and staff to implement them.

If you want to work with athletes, it is helpful to have some coaching experience as well as some contacts who are coaches. You might consider offering a free workout to various teams so the children and parents can see what you are about. If you have connections in a school system, you could go into schools or to team practices and speak to the athletes about what you do. Then send them home with information for their parents. Parents must feel that your services are essential to their children's success, because they are so busy it will be an effort to fit your training into their schedules.

Creating Success in a Competitive Market

Success is a relative term, and means something different to everyone. It may be the number of programs you run, your profit margin, or the measurable difference you make in the lives of the children you coach. Here success will mean all of those things. In order to make a good living, you will need to run multiple programs with good participation. Proper pricing is also important. If you price too low, you will not make a profit. If you price too high, parents will not pay for their children to participate. Finally, the more marked improvement in the participants of your programs, the more likely they will return and bring other clients with them.

Because there is currently such a buzz about youth fitness, you will have a lot of competition for clients. Do some research and find out the locations of your competitors in the community. Your competitors may not necessarily be running programs like yours; they're anyone who may compete with you for program members. Any organized movement programs should be examined. Look into the specifics of each program and figure out ways to set yours apart.

E ssential

You are competing for the parents' time and money. Your biggest competition for these commodities will not be other trainers, it will be the people putting on soccer, football, field hockey, lacrosse, or other sports-skills camps. Additionally, you are also competing with any other activity that drains families' valuable resources.

Because there is a high turnover rate for participants in these types of programs, you'll constantly need to network, advertise, and upgrade your programs if you wish to remain successful. Develop a mailing list to keep your clients informed of what you are doing. E-mail is the least expensive and quickest form of communication, but every so often you should actually send a flyer or post card by snail mail. The lives of young people are constantly changing, and athletes who participate in one session may not return for various reasons. They graduate, move, switch sports, and change interests rather quickly, so you will constantly need to find new clients.

Designing and Implementing Safe Programs

Safety is always a primary consideration for trainers, but it is especially important when dealing with children. Even if you have experience training and coaching young people, it would be wise to do some reading and/or take a course on training children. Because they are still growing, children require special consideration. Avery Faigenbaum is a leading researcher and expert in this field. He has published numerous articles and books on training children, and has also made videos and lectured around the country on this topic. His work is a tremendous resource for program design and can be found on Amazon.com or at any large bookstore.

 **Alert**

To ensure that you are covered in the event of injury or some other accident, have an attorney examine your liability waiver and health questionnaire. Be vigilant in having each participant complete forms prior to participation. Review them carefully and keep them on hand at every session in case you need emergency information.

Before beginning a training program, it is important to require parents to complete and sign a thorough health questionnaire and liability waiver. While most children you work with will be healthy, they may have issues such as asthma, allergies, or diabetes that you need to be aware of. You also want to cover yourself in the event that they have an unknown underlying condition that manifests during your sessions. The bottom line is that you need to protect both yourself and your participants.

Training the High School Athlete

Much of what is true for youth training programs also applies to training high school athletes. Their parents play a large role in the decision-making process, and you will still have a great deal of competition for clients. Once again, you will need liability waivers and medical history forms completed and signed prior to participation. If you enjoy working with this age group, you may consider whether you would like to work in a school setting or develop programs outside of the school.

Special Considerations for This Age Group

There are several differences between training youth and adolescents. One obvious difference is a higher level of athletic ability. High school athletes are more physically developed and can be pushed harder than younger athletes. At the adolescent age, you may also have to discipline more frequently. It is helpful to clearly explain the rules and consequences of non-compliance from the start to minimize disruptions and decrease distractions.

At this age, athletes become increasingly aware of the immense amount of hard work, dedication, and time that true athletic success requires. Some will be willing to rise to the challenge, and others will have more of an, "I want results now" mentality. This latter group may become interested in all kinds of performance-enhancing aids. Be prepared to be bombarded with questions pertaining to ergogenic aids both legal and illegal. Educating yourself on the benefits and risks of commonly used performance enhancers will help you have productive conversations, and will increase the athletes' respect for you. You might use this as an opportunity to discuss and promote natural supplements such as protein powders, energy drinks, and vitamins. If you have a specific product line you find effective, you can sell and earn passive income.

Employment in a School System

High school strength coaches are typically employed as physical education teachers. They are then given a stipend to work as a strength coach after school. Because of unions, it is difficult to become a high school strength coach if you are not also a teacher. However, in private or parochial schools, it is more likely to be an option. High schools offer nice benefits if you are lucky enough to be employed full time, including extensive vacation time and relatively short work hours.

 Fact

Do not be naïve. High school athletes do use performance-enhancing drugs. In 2003, an estimated 2–5 percent of high school athletes had tried anabolic steroids to enhance athletic performance. This number continues to rise, and it is the responsibility of coaches and trainers to educate their athletes on the perils of using these drugs.

If there are schools in your area that do not yet use the services of a strength coach, you can approach them as an independent contractor. You can present to them the services you may offer, and remind them that as an independent contractor they will save money by not paying your benefits.

Offering Services Outside of Schools

If you wish to work with the high school population but not be employed in the school system, you may do so in a couple of different ways. You can market yourself to the athletes themselves and work with them individually to improve performance. This is great if you can accomplish it, but again, it may be a tough sell due to financial considerations. Another option is to approach coaches and sell team strength and conditioning programs designed specifically for their sport.

You may choose to offer a variety of services, including but not limited to, strength programs, conditioning programs, testing, lecturing, pregame agility warm-ups, and off-season, in-season, or preseason workouts. Contact the athletic directors at each school and make them aware of the services you are offering. Start with a letter, then follow up with a phone call. They may promote you to their coaches or provide you with a way to contact them. The coaches may, in turn, use money in their budgets to hire you or promote you to the parents of their athletes.

Scheduling

Scheduling time to work with high school athletes can be quite challenging. The only time you can train them is after school, on the weekends, or during school vacations. Even then, chances are they will have other commitments such as practices and games that you will have to work around. Remember that most of your athletes will not be able to drive themselves, so they will need to rely on their parents or older siblings. Many student athletes are already overbooked and exhausted, so you will really have to demonstrate to them and their parents why your services are necessary.

Most of your business will be generated during after-school hours, 2:30–8 P.M. Remember that students will also need time to complete homework, and will likely be relying on their parents for rides.

College- and University-Level Athletes

The college training market is much more difficult to tap into. You need a higher level of education and more experience than you would in working with the general population. There is also more pressure at this level, because your performance directly affects the livelihood of others.

Becoming a College Strength and Conditioning Coach

In order to become a college strength and conditioning coach, you will generally need at least a bachelor's degree in some type of exercise science. A master's degree is often preferred. You will also typically be required to be certified as a strength and conditioning specialist (CSCS) from the National Strength and Conditioning

Association, and/or have certifications through the USAW or the Collegiate Strength and Conditioning Coaches Association. In addition, most schools require prior experience through either a graduate assistantship or internship. The NCAA lists job opportunities along with their requirements on its Web site at *www.ncaa.org.*

E ssential

Working as a college strength coach is both challenging and rewarding. There is a good deal of pressure to prevent injuries and improve athletic performance. At this level, other peoples' jobs are affected by how well you perform your job. You will put in a great deal of time and effort, though the pay may not reflect the extensive time commitment.

Marketing to College Athletes

Becoming a strength coach at a college or university requires a great deal of education and planning. It also requires a tremendous amount of time and energy. Some people enjoy this lifestyle, but it is certainly not for everyone. If you wish to work with this population but do not want to be employed by an institution of higher education, you may choose to create your own programs and work with college athletes individually or in groups. This is a relatively small market, but it can be tapped into.

Summer will be your most profitable and busiest time, as college students are home and away from their coaches and trainers. They will usually have a workout program from their college coach to be performed while they are on break. You may choose to work within this program or develop a complementary program of your own. Whatever you choose, the athlete must be ready for his season when he returns to school.

College students often do not have the finances to afford individual training sessions, so your best bet is promoting small or large group training. Because this is a small, specialized market and will likely only make up a portion of your income, it would not be financially sound to spend a lot of money on advertising. You may find it easiest to begin working with athletes in high school and continue when they get to the college level. You might also network with college coaches who may refer their athletes to you for the summer. Finally, you could hang flyers and place brochures in places frequented by college students.

Training with Professional Athletes

Competition for professional training jobs is extremely intense. Your knowledge base and experience must be quite extensive in order to work at this level. This is a very small market and a highly demanding job. You will be required to keep long hours and travel a great deal. However, it is also a very exciting and rewarding job with many perks.

Are You Qualified?

In order to even be considered for a professional strength-coaching position, you must have extensive credentials and experience. Most jobs require a master's degree or higher, as well as certification by the NSCA as a certified strength and conditioning specialist. Many clubs require you to have worked in the minor leagues or at a Division I college. At this level, you will not only be supervising their strength training, you will likely be involved in conditioning programs and nutrition as well.

How Do You Break into the Market?

The truth is, people do not typically break into this market, they climb. They have put in many long hours throughout their careers to make it to this level. Most professional strength coaches have moved up through the ranks, starting at the college level. They begin as graduate assistant coaches, then move to assistant then head college coach. A very few may be lucky enough to know someone and skip a few rungs in the ladder, but this is not common.

Special Considerations for the Professional Athlete

When interacting with professional athletes, you are dealing with significant physical and mental considerations. Because they are always in the public eye, there is a high level of stress. Privacy and confidentiality are of the utmost importance. There is a great deal at stake at this level, so proper program design is imperative. You never want to cause an athlete to be injured or retard their progress in returning from an injury. Your programs will vary based on a number of factors, such as age of the athlete, workout history, injuries, the sport and position they play, level of motivation, and current physical condition. You can make or break an athlete's career if safety is not practiced at all times.

Remember that your weekend warrior clients were once athletes. Many times they will believe they can still do what they did twenty or thirty years before. The fact is, they are older and their bodies cannot handle the same type of abuse. Be sure to train safely while providing enough of a challenge so that they do not get frustrated or bored.

Training the Weekend Warrior

Weekend warriors are adults who were active and athletic when they were younger, but now intermittently play sports for recreation. They may be a part of an organized team or simply play pick-up games with their friends. Even though they are not as young as they once were, most adult athletes still want to excel at whatever sport they are playing, and as an adult they may now have the financial resources to be able to hire a trainer. You can help your client to both improve their game and to generally feel better. The weekend warrior is a great group to work with, but they have some special considerations. For example, this group will have more health concerns because they are older. They will tend to have and be prone to more injuries and illnesses, and will also recover more slowly because they are older, and may be less consistent with their workouts.

Why Sports-Specific Training for the Weekend Warrior?

This type of training increases your clients' functionality. It allows them to move more fluidly and comfortably. Sports-specific training transfers more easily to activities of daily life. Traditional weight training has its place but does not transfer as directly to the playing field. The weekend warrior needs cardiovascular conditioning, agility, flexibility, and speed to perform to their maximum potential.

Many adults prefer sports training because they find it to be more fun and interesting than traditional training. Sports training makes the time pass more quickly, and has more cardiovascular benefits than traditional weight training. That being said, it is also not for everyone.

Chapter 7

Starting Your Personal-Training Career

At this point, you should have the education and certification that you need, and be familiar with the various settings where you might work. Ideally, you will also have some experience through schooling, shadowing, or internship. Your next step will be finding a job and building your clientele. These tasks will take time, effort, and determination. By being prepared, making a plan, and following through, you should be able to create a successful career.

Looking for a Job

There are many things to consider when looking for a job. Ideally, you will work in a place that you find enjoyable, that fits your philosophy of personal training, and that provides desirable hours and compensation. However, bear in mind that if this is your first job, you may have to take what you can get for a while. Just as in any career, you will need to pay your dues. Therefore, try to be realistic, and find a job where you can gain as much experience as possible so you can develop your skills. If your dream job falls in your lap then take it, but be reasonable with your expectations and demands.

Where Do You Want to Work?

Before you start looking for a job, you must decide where you want to work. You should now be familiar with the basic differences between working in a health club, a studio, and in corporate fitness. Which, if any, do you find appealing? A major consideration is whether or not you need benefits. If you do need benefits, your options of where to apply will likely be limited to a large health club or corporate fitness. It is also helpful at this point to consider where you want to be in five years. What are your short- and long-term professional goals? Your goals will help dictate the types of businesses to which you apply. If you are hoping to open your own studio in the future, then it makes sense to gain experience working in a studio. If you simply want to be a trainer for a few years while you work toward doing something else, then you can work pretty much anywhere that pays what you are looking for. If you want to gain the most experience you can in the shortest amount of time, a health club is a good place to start, because you come in contact with large numbers of potential clients daily.

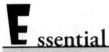

Your first job will be an entry-level position. You can expect to start at the bottom and work your way up. Gain as much experience as possible and focus on developing your personal training skills. Introduce yourself to many different people and situations to broaden your knowledge base.

Locating Job Opportunities

There are many ways to find a job as a personal trainer. If you had a shadowing experience or performed some type of internship that you enjoyed, you might inquire about whether that facility is hiring. You can also use the person you shadowed as a resource. Because that person has been in the business, chances are he knows more people and places that may be looking for a trainer. Another wise place to look for job opportunities is the organization through which you obtained your certification. Many of these organizations now have jobs posted on their Web sites. If you attended a college or university, you may be able to find leads there through your former professors or the career services department. An online search and the newspaper classifieds may also provide you with leads. Finally, you might consider going directly to businesses in your area to see if they are hiring.

Once you have decided where you will apply, send out your resume. Include a cover letter explaining what job you are applying for and why you feel you should be hired for the position. About a week later, follow up with a phone call. Confirm that your resume has been received and inquire about when they will begin interviewing.

Preparing for an Interview

There is quite a bit of preparation required for job interviews. Start out by researching the business where you will interview. Learn how long it has been in business and if it is corporately or privately owned. Other important facts to research are the costs of memberships, the number of full- and part-time trainers, and how much of a role personal training plays in their business. If possible, obtain a complete job description well before your interview. Practice your answers to some typical interview questions: How would you describe yourself? What are your career goals? What do you feel are your strengths and weaknesses? Why did you choose this career?

Question

Is it more beneficial to work in a large, corporate-owned club or a small, family owned club?
If you are just starting out, you need maximum face-to-face time with clients of different ability levels. A large, corporate-owned club will provide you with a diverse population with whom you can practice and hone your skills.

Go into the interview prepared to ask thoughtful questions, such as: How have you improved the facility in the past and what improvements do you have planned for the future? How many members do you have? What percentage of your members hires personal trainers? How do you compensate your trainers? On average, how many clients do the trainers work with? Are there different levels of trainers? Do you give bonuses? What type of training do you give your trainers? Do you pay for continuing education? Do trainers have to work desk hours? Learning this information will give you a feel for your potential to be successful as a trainer in that establishment.

Proper dress for an interview is an important factor in making a good impression. While you may be working in sneakers and exercise clothes, they are inappropriate for an interview. At a minimum, men should wear a shirt and tie and women a blouse and dress pants or a skirt. It is better to be overdressed than underdressed for an interview.

 Fact

Most interviewers know whether or not they will hire the interviewee within the first thirty seconds of meeting them. This is where a good first impression makes all the difference. You need to portray confidence, be prepared, and separate yourself from the rest of the interview pool.

Obtaining Your First Client

Finding your first client may be daunting and difficult, or it could happen without much effort. Because personal training is becoming increasingly popular, trainers are hot commodities. Nowadays, people are fascinated by personal training and personal trainers. Get your name out in the market any way you can. Let people know you are now certified and beginning to work as a trainer. Have your friends and family tell their friends. Your first client is out there, and should not be too hard to find.

Will Your Employer Help You?

If you are employed by a health club, gym, or studio, your employer should assist you in finding clients. There is typically a system in place where new members are offered personal-training services and introduced to a trainer. The club may offer a free orientation session or a discounted training package for people who join. While you cannot count on this system for all of your clients, it should help you obtain a few people with whom you can get started.

E ssential

Now you are the new trainer in town. Some members will need some time to warm up to you, and others will want to get to know you right away. Be careful not to poach clients from any of the other trainers. Always ask potential clients if they are currently working with another trainer. Taking clients from other trainers is a sure way to start off on the wrong foot.

Your employer should also place or allow you to post a photo and bio in a prominent location so that current members may learn about and choose to train with you. This may be in the form of a newsletter, brochure, or flyer. The more visible you are, the more likely you'll be to attract clients.

Start with Friends and Family

Since your biggest supporters are likely to be your friends and family, you might consider starting with them as your first clients. There is already an element of trust and respect in most cases, so this makes sense. Send out a letter to everyone you know announcing and explaining your new career. You may choose to offer a discount to your family and friends, but make sure they understand that your time is valuable. If they are not interested in training with you themselves, ask them to refer you to people they know who may be interested.

Special Offers to Gain Clients

Because you lack experience and need to attract people to work with, you may want to offer a lower rate as you are starting out, if your employer allows it. This should only be a slightly reduced rate;

no more than 10–20 percent less than the more experienced trainers. For example, if the veteran trainers at your club charge $50 per hour, you could charge $40 for the first three to six months, then increase to $45 or $50. Your approach will depend on how quickly your business grows. The more booked your schedule gets, the more you can charge for your services.

E ssential

Offering discounted sessions is okay initially, but should be done with caution. Discounting your fees too much for too long may lessen the perceived value of your services compared with other trainers.

Another way to increase your clientele is to offer your current clients incentives for referring new clients to you. You may offer current clients a free session if they refer someone to you who buys a package. Again, the generosity of your offers will depend on how badly you are in need of new clients. You may only offer 25 percent or 50 percent off the next session for a referral, if your schedule is pretty full.

Developing Your Warm Market

Whether you like it or not, personal training is sales. You may be the best personal trainer in the world, but if you cannot sell, your success will be limited. In order to develop and maintain a client base, you must sell your services. This is much easier to accomplish if you establish a sizeable warm market. Your warm market consists of anyone with whom you have some type of relationship. You may only have met them once, but they know who you are. It is much easier to cultivate trust and then make a sale when you already have some type of rapport. Therefore, any way you can increase your warm market is advantageous.

Don't Sell Like a Salesperson

People do not like to be sold to. They do however enjoy buying things. The key is to figure out how to make people want to buy your services without feeling like they are being sold to. This is best accomplished by establishing relationships. Be friendly and open with the people you meet and interact with during the course of your day. Ask lots of questions so you can really get to know people. Genuinely listen to what they are saying and try to hear in it what they need that you can provide. For example, if someone complains of back pain, let her know that by strengthening her core, she can decrease or eliminate back pain. Give them enough information to pique their interest, so that they start asking questions of you. At that point, you can offer your services.

 Question

How can I sell if I have no background in sales?
There are numerous ways to learn sales. Your local small business association is a great place to start. They may offer or direct you to workshops and tutorials on this subject. If you enjoy reading, visit your local library or bookstore to locate books about sales techniques. You may also consider taking some college business courses.

It is important to feel comfortable discussing with people exactly what you do and why they need your services. In the beginning, you may find it helpful to have a brief statement prepared so you know what to say and are confident and concise. Be enthusiastic and excited. Make it fun for people to talk to you, so they will realize that they will enjoy working with you as well. Help them see that you are an invaluable resource for their fitness and wellness needs; you can assist them in reaching their goals in a safe and enjoyable way.

Appealing to Their Senses

When promoting any service, you need to appeal to the senses of the people to whom you are selling. Find out why they are considering personal training. Is it because they are overweight, wish to train for something, want to feel better, or is there some other reason? Obtain this information within the first minute of your conversation and turn it into your selling point. Take what they have told you and use it to demonstrate the value of your services. Take into consideration the emotional aspects of what they are saying and use it to emphasize that you can provide what they need.

People are generally resistant to change. Most people will have excuses about why they cannot or do not have time for exercise. Oftentimes, you will encounter people who have tried and failed over and over to make exercise a consistent part of their lives. In many cases, you will need to do some gentle persuading to convince people that they can be successful with you as their trainer. If you are truly good at what you do, once they have had their initial appointment, they will want to keep coming back.

E ssential

Make a second appointment as soon as your new client has completed the first session. If they are not interested in training weekly, tell them they can train monthly. Set up the appointment before they leave. If you fail to do so, there is a good chance they will not rebook with you, as other things will get in the way.

If money is an issue for someone, suggest that they share the session with a friend and split the cost. Bartering is another solution. Some potential clients may provide a service that you could use, such as hairdressers, massage therapists, landscapers, printers, etc. If that person is interested and you can agree on a fair trade, you could exchange services instead of money. Another option is to sell gift certificates for your services that people could give to someone wishing to train with you for a birthday, anniversary, or other occasion.

Closing the Sale

The most important concept in sales is follow up. You will often not sell an appointment the first or even second time you approach a potential client. The key is to continually plant seeds by demonstrating to people the benefits of hiring you. Keep your name in the forefront of their minds, so when they are ready to hire a trainer they think of and contact you. Keep a list of potential prospects and important information about them. Many times people will contact you about training and then disappear. A simple follow-up call or e-mail may get them focused, and they will book an appointment. Another common occurrence is that people you train once a month or less will say they will call for another appointment, but then they get busy and forget. A gentle reminder call will cause them to schedule another appointment. Be persistent, but do not chase people. You need to find a balance where you are reminding people to make appointments, but not forcing or pestering them.

Your Training Philosophy and Style

Developing a philosophy and training style should be a conscious, mindful process. It is important to know what you believe in and base your methods on, so you can confidently convey this to both current and potential clients. Your approach to training is uniquely yours and will set you apart from other professionals. It will have a major impact on the clientele you attract. As you gain experience, your approach will change and grow over time.

Creating Your Philosophy

Many factors will influence your philosophy and the way you work with your clients. Your own exercise history will play a large role, as will your personality, nutritional habits, educational background, and more. If you are unsure of how to verbalize what you believe, answering the following questions will get you started in the right direction:

- How hard and how often do you feel your clients should exercise?
- What types of exercise do you recommend?
- Do you enjoy nurturing or do you prefer to push clients to the limit?
- In a weight loss program, do you emphasize cardiovascular exercise, nutrition, or both?

While it is important to have a strong sense of who you are and what you believe, it is also important to be flexible. To a certain extent, you will need to adapt your style to what your clients want and need or you will lose people.

Incorporate your philosophy into your sales presentations. Be up front with people about how you work with your clients to meet their needs. Give specific examples to demonstrate how your particular style has been effective.

How to Develop a Niche

In order to be successful in this competitive market, you need to create a niche. A niche is a specialization that sets you apart from the competition. It is one reason that people will sign up with you and not one of the many other trainers around. A niche is something that you will develop throughout your career as you gain experience and make a name for yourself. However, it does not need to be a happy accident. Rather, you should actively work to create a niche for yourself sooner rather than later.

Making the Most of Your Strengths

When finding or choosing a niche, there are two main considerations: your strengths as a trainer and the aspects of training that you most enjoy. Hopefully these two things will be the same, or at least share some commonalities. Start with the type of client with whom you prefer to work. It may be males or females, athletes or weekend warriors, young people or the elderly. You may enjoy working with people who battle eating issues, have physical disabilities, or have no real preference.

Next, figure out where your strengths lie, whether they are in weight loss programs, body building, injury rehabilitation, or something else entirely. Keep in mind throughout this process that you should not be putting yourself in a box or limiting yourself to a very small specialization. You may be able to specialize once you are established, but in the beginning of your career it is not beneficial to limit yourself too much.

You may find it helpful when choosing your niche to survey your current clients. Ask them what they feel are your strengths and why they feel that way. Talk to your friends and family as well. You may discover strengths you did not realize you possessed.

 Fact

Baby Boomers make up the largest percentage of our population and have the most discretionary income. It is estimated that 50 percent have hypertension, 40 percent are overweight, and 25 percent smoke. Making a niche with this population could be quite profitable.

Promotion of a Specialty

Some trainers fall into a niche through the natural course of their careers. They help someone rehabilitate a knee injury and suddenly they are the "knee guru," or they work with an athlete who goes on to the Olympics and become known as the local "sports performance specialist." While these situations do occur, they are often as rare as winning the lottery. Why leave your career to chance? Consciously create your niche and take every opportunity to present yourself as a specialist in whatever you have chosen. Do be sure that you are legitimately qualified in the area you claim as your specialty. If you never played a sport in your life, it is unlikely that you will be the best sports trainer around.

Making a Name for Yourself

There are numerous ways to become known as a personal trainer. One way is to have clients obtain visible success. As people begin seeing positive changes in your clients, your credibility will rise. Volunteering in the area will also help get your name out there. You want to put yourself in front of as many people as possible, as often as possible. Show people who you are, what you know, and what you can do.

Creating Success Stories

As a personal trainer, you will assist people in many ways. You will help them become stronger, have more endurance, decrease joint pain, lower cholesterol and blood pressure, and much more. These are all great accomplishments, and will help you retain your current clients. However, obvious physical changes in your clients will help you gain more clients. As your clients lose weight and build muscle, others will see this and want to do the same. They will see that working out with you yields positive physical changes.

Effecting physical changes is important, and that is why the majority of your clients will retain your services. Your clients will also experience emotional changes, and they are just as important, if not more important, than physical changes. They may feel happier, more confident, more positive, etc. You can capitalize on their emotional high by asking them to refer their friends and family. They will want to share their enthusiasm with others, and in turn you could find yourself with an increase in clientele.

Your Clients Are Your Best Advertisement

You can capitalize on your success with your clients by putting their stories in brochures and flyers. Have them tell in their own words how you have helped them. Show before and after pictures if they are comfortable with that. In exchange, you may consider offering them a free session. Be respectful of your clients' privacy, and obtain permission prior to using their names, pictures or stories.

Sharing success stories can generate interest from people looking to achieve similar goals. Be sure to include several different accomplishments so you do not create the impression that working with you will only produce a specific result. If all of your featured clients lost weight, you may not get the attention of someone looking to train for a marathon. Instead, include a story about weight loss and another about a client who completed an endurance race such as a triathlon.

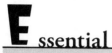

Volunteering Within the Community

Volunteering is a great way to increase your name recognition and establish relationships within the community. There are unlimited ways to volunteer in the community. You could sit on a committee to end hunger, or perform fundraising for a special cause. You could also help out at road races, bike races, or walk-a-thons, but do not need to limit yourself to the health and fitness realm. Focus on places frequented by the populations with whom you wish to work.

Chapter 8

Setting Up Your Business

Starting a business from scratch can be a daunting task. It requires a tremendous amount of vision, determination, and money. Planning is a key component to success. If you do not plan adequately and put that plan in writing, your venture is doomed to failure. It is also wise to employ the services of an accountant who can assist you in setting up the financial aspects of your business. Whether you are renting space in an existing facility or opening a place of your own, you will take similar steps to get your business up and running.

Importance of a Business Plan

A business plan is a document containing specific information about your company, your industry, and the future of both. Writing a business plan is time-consuming, but is vastly important, because one greatly increases your probability of success.

Business plans serve three purposes. The first is communication. If you wish to attract investors or secure a loan, your business plan will communicate to potential investors where you are going and how you plan to get there. In fact, it is quite difficult to obtain financing for your company without a business plan. A second function of a business plan is tracking, monitoring, and evaluating your progress over the short and long term. In fact, the business plan is a great tool with which to chart and gauge your growth. Keep in mind that your plan is not set in stone and will continually change and evolve over time. Finally, a business plan assists you in planning for the future.

With proper research, you will be able to use your plan to project and avoid any pitfalls or obstacles that may arise.

Alert

If you are opening or starting your own business, a business plan is a must. Financial institutions and private investors will not even consider funding your project without seeing a concrete plan. Banks will take some risk, but they need to see financial projections, and want to know that you are adequately prepared for the endeavor.

What to Include in Your Business Plan

While there is not one right way to create a business plan, most contain similar types of information. Start with a cover page and table of contents so the information inside is easier to locate. Next, you should include an executive summary. The executive summary is a one-to-two-page document that summarizes the business plan. It is included so people do not need to read the entire document if they so choose. While the executive summary is placed in the front of your plan, it is easier to write once you have completed all of the other sections. The other information generally included in a business plan includes a description of your business and the services you will provide, market analysis, information on owners and personnel, competition, financial information, and a marketing plan. The appendix should include tax returns from the past three years, a copy of the lease agreement, your resume, and any other legal documents. The most important factor for a successful business plan is that the information is clear, thorough, and accurate.

Helpful Resources for Creating Your Business Plan

Many books, articles, software, and Web sites have been devoted to the topic of creating a business plan. A simple Google search for "writing a business plan" will provide you with dozens of helpful resources, as will a search on Amazon.com. For free advice, try *www.business.gov*, click on "Launching" then on "Task 3 Writing a

Business Plan." This invaluable resource includes detailed information on writing business plans, sample business plans, frequently asked questions, an interactive business planner, and much more. There is even a link to a thorough online business-plan writing workshop.

Question

Where can I get help writing my plan in person?
If you need personal assistance, visit your local Small Business Association (SBA) or Chamber of Commerce. The SBA is usually staffed by retired executives and business owners who have many years of knowledge and experience to share. They offer free advice on developing and writing your business plan, as well as a great deal of other valuable information.

If you feel you need more help with your plan, you can log on to bplans.com. There you can find free advice or purchase software called Business Plan Pro from Palo Alto Software. The software will walk you through writing a business plan step by step. It checks your financial information for accuracy and your overall data for comprehensiveness. It also allows you to export the data to programs such as Microsoft Word, Excel, and PowerPoint. In addition, you'll receive free technical support.

Choosing the Structure of Your Business

There are several ways you may choose to organize your new business, including sole proprietorship, partnership, incorporation, or LLC. How you structure your business will determine the extent of your legal liability and decision-making capabilities. It will also affect how you are taxed and what write-offs you may take. Before you make a choice, you need to be clear about the advantages and disadvantages of each form of ownership.

Sole Proprietorships and Partnerships

Sole proprietorships and partnerships are similar entities, legally speaking. In a sole proprietorship, the business is owned by one individual who is personally liable for all debts and lawsuits against the business. In a partnership, the ownership and liability are shared by two or more people. The advantage of establishing these types of businesses is that they are simpler and less expensive to organize than corporations. They can be a convenient way to start out if you are working as an independent contractor in someone else's space, or are planning on keeping your business a part-time operation. However, there are significant disadvantages to a trainer who chooses this form of ownership. The main disadvantage being that you can be personally sued if one of your clients is injured. Also, in the event that your business gets into financial trouble, you could lose your financial well-being, as you are completely responsible for all debts. Finally, you will be required to pay self-employment tax as a sole proprietor, which you do not have to do as a corporation.

E ssential

Start off on the right foot by hiring an accountant to help you choose the right business structure for your situation. Setting up your business properly will save you a great deal of time and money. It will also help you avoid getting into trouble with the government.

Corporations

A corporation is, by law, a separate legal entity. Shareholders invest but are not responsible for the corporation's liabilities. Any lawsuits would be filed against the corporation and not its shareholders, and therefore, personal assets are protected. C corporations are the most common, and are allowed an unlimited number of shareholders. The disadvantage of C corporations is the double tax. The business and the shareholders are both taxed. An S corporation has a different tax structure, so the corporation itself is not taxed, only the shareholders. An S corporation is limited to seventy-five shareholders, but it is unlikely that a personal training business would require even close to that number.

Fact

If an individual establishes a sole proprietorship that makes a profit of $200,000 in a year, he will pay taxes on the full amount. However, if his business was an S corporation, he could put himself on the payroll for $100,000 and take the remainder as a distribution. By doing this, he does not have to pay Social Security or Medicare on half of his income.

If you choose to incorporate, your first step is to hire an attorney. Each state has different laws, and it is important to follow the correct procedures so you are not fined. Initially, you will file as a C corporation, and then file more paperwork to change to an S corporation. Typically, you will pay $500–$700 in lawyer's fees, plus a filing fee to the Secretary of State office. While this may seem like a big expense, it pays off in decreased personal liability and tax benefits. It is also much easier to obtain financing when your company is incorporated, so if you are planning to open your own place, this is likely what your accountant will recommend.

Limited Liability Companies

Limited Liability Companies (LLCs) are a relatively new entity. They are a cross between partnerships and corporations. They are similar to corporations in that the liability lies with the business, but there is more flexibility with ownership than in corporations. You can establish yourself in your state as an LLC and elect to be taxed as an S corporation by the IRS to avoid being double taxed. It is also a good idea to state your business as an LLC in case you decide later to bring on another partner. The tax laws do get a bit more complicated with LLCs, and the laws are different in every state, so be sure to consult an attorney regarding the laws in your state.

Record Keeping

Keeping proper records is essential to running any successful business. First and foremost, adequate record keeping is required by law for tax purposes. In addition to the legal considerations, record keeping allows you to track and measure growth and address issues as they arise. The better and more accurately you keep your records, the less you will spend in the long run on accounting and legal fees.

Financial Records

There are several types of financial records you will need to keep: sales records, cash receipts, accounts payable, and accounts receivable. The simplest and least expensive way to keep these records is by hand. If you choose to go this route, your accountant can set you up with a system of ledgers that works for you. If you find you are spending too much time with the books, you may choose to purchase financial software that is relatively inexpensive and easy to use. There are generic programs such as Intuit's QuickBooks and Peachtree Accounting that will assist you with invoicing, accounts receivable, accounts payable, etc. The appeal is that you enter the data and the software performs the calculations. There is less chance of error with this method. These programs also make it easy to print reports for your accountant, and may ultimately keep your accounting costs down.

If you are opening your own facility, more specialized programs specific to personal training are also available. These companies charge a monthly fee, but there is often no charge for the software itself. They provide many services, including: Electronic Funds Transfer (EFT) and credit card processing; billing; collections on delinquent accounts; member check in; membership card services; guest and prospect tracking; session tracking; renewal notices; and much more. Several of these companies are listed below, but there are numerous companies offering these services, so do your research and find the best value for your business.

Twin Oaks	*www.tosd.com*
eFit Financial	*www.efitfinancial.com*

ABC Financial	✍www.abcfinancial.com
ASF International	✍www.asfint.com
CSI Software	✍www.csisoftwareusa.com

The size of your business and cost of the system will likely be the major considerations when deciding upon a method of record keeping. If you are unsure where to begin, consult with your accountant.

 Question

How can I know which software product will work best for my company?
First, look at whether or not the program meets your anticipated needs. Then project the amount of business you will be producing and determine if the product is affordable. Most companies will send you a demo disk or refer you to a business in the area that uses their product so you can see firsthand how it works and if it is right for you.

Client Records

Each client or member should have her own file. These files should contain copies of the membership application, medical history forms, informed consent, results of exercise testing, signed contracts, goal sheets, and past and current exercise programs. In order to protect confidentiality, all documents should be kept locked in a place where only you and the personnel of your choice have access.

Keeping accurate client records is important for two reasons. The first is professionalism. It looks extremely unprofessional if you can't locate results of prior testing or an old exercise program. By keeping all documents in one place, everything will be in order and at your fingertips. Keeping careful track of your clients and their progress may seem like a lot of work, but in the long run it will make for less work and a smoother-running business. You will be able to develop and implement programs and chart progress much more effectively if you are organized.

The second reason to keep accurate client records is legal liability. In the event of a lawsuit, you can produce the informed consent and medical history forms, as well as exactly what exercise programs the client had been instructed to perform. Providing proper documentation demonstrates responsibility and professionalism and gives the lawyer something to work with.

Budgeting

Whether you are renting space in an existing facility or opening a facility of your own, you will need to create and follow a budget. A budget provides you with a plan and helps monitor the status of your business. It is a work in progress and will constantly need to be modified and updated.

E ssential

If a client stops training with you for a period of time and starts again, you can refer to their old file and update any new information instead of starting from scratch. By examining their old programs, you can get them started back on the right path much more easily.

Your budget needs to balance income and expenses. The fewer expenses you have, the simpler your budget. You may want to have both monthly and yearly budgets. The nature of the personal training business requires the budget to be fluid, as different times of year tend to bring more or less business. Initially, your budget will require some guesswork. Draw on past experiences and your research as much as possible to increase your accuracy. You may need to use a range of numbers or create best and worst case scenario budgets. The more budgets you create, the better you will become.

If you are opening your own facility, your budget will likely include the following expenses: lease or rent, utilities, insurance, advertising, repairs and maintenance, taxes, salaries, office supplies, accounting and legal fees, and depreciation of equipment. Your income will be from memberships, personal training, and possibly rent from other trainers. If you choose to sell nutritional or other products in your facility, they will also need to be accounted for in the budget. If you are renting space or working in-home, you will have similar categories of expenses, but the numbers will be smaller. Your income will pretty much come from personal training and maybe product sales.

Taxes and Your Accountant

People choose to use or not use accountants for a variety of reasons. However, the fact is they are a great asset to any business owner and can save you a great deal of time, money, and hassle. The services of an accountant are particularly important when starting a business, so you get off on the right foot. If you begin with the proper systems, you will not have to fix expensive mistakes later on.

Alert

Just as you are an expert at training people, accountants are experts in the area of taxes. It would be foolish for an accountant to try to develop a training program for a body builder. In the same way, it is foolish for trainers to try to handle their taxes on their own.

Advantages to Using an Accountant

The major advantage to using an accountant is that you are dealing with a professional who is trained to handle the financial aspects of your business. As a personal trainer, it is likely you have very little financial background. Accountants help with bookkeeping and measuring the progress of your business. They also keep up with rapidly changing tax laws. It is a simple fact that people who use accountants claim more deductions on their tax returns than those who file themselves. Tax laws are so complex, that even with computer programs you may omit important information and deductions.

Hiring an Accountant

There are many ways one may utilize an accountant. If you are just starting out, you may choose to consult an accountant and have them set up your record-keeping systems. Then you may not see them again until tax time. As your business grows, you may find you need your accountant on a monthly basis. There will come a point where it is no longer profitable for you to spend your time keeping books. You will focus on getting more business while your accountant watches the bottom line, makes sure you are complying with the ever-changing tax laws, and monitors the growth of your business.

Not all accountants are equal. They, like any professional, have varied amounts of experience, charge different rates, and have varied work ethics. Your best bet is to interview several people to see who best fits with your own philosophy, style, and budget.

Hiring Help

If you are just getting your business started, you may choose not to hire employees right away. However, as your business grows, you may eventually need people to work for you. Depending on the size of your facility, you may need janitorial staff, front desk or office staff, maintenance, or other trainers. There are many practical and legal considerations involved in being an employer.

Choosing Who to Hire

When hiring people to work for you, you need to consider more than just their professional qualifications. Your employees are an extension of you. In order to have a harmonious work environment, you need to hire people whose attitudes and behaviors fall in line with your own standards and values. The people you hire should be team players who put the well-being of the business before their personal interests. When every member of the team works toward the same goals, everyone wins. The business thrives, and therefore the employees thrive. They should also be willing to accept constructive criticism and learn from others. An employee who is unwilling to modify the way they do things is difficult to deal with and will end up being a detriment

It is difficult to assess character from an interview alone, though asking in-depth, probing questions can help. Give the interviewee some "what if" scenarios and ask how they would handle them. Provided you receive honest answers, these will give you a feel for their nature and personality. Confirming the accuracy of the applicant's resume is a must. Verify that the prospect has all of the credentials and experience he claims to have. Call every reference provided and be prepared to ask questions about your potential employee's character. Finally, observing the potential employee interacting with members and staff will also provide valuable information about whether or not he will mesh with your business.

Employees and Independent Contractors

There are major differences between hiring employees and paying independent contractors. When you hire an employee, you must contribute half of the Social Security and Medicare taxes. You also need to carry worker's compensation insurance and pay into unemployment. This can add up to significant expenses. If you hire someone as an independent contractor, you are only responsible for paying her fee and filing a 1099 form with the IRS.

Because it is less costly to hire someone as an independent contractor, it is attractive to business owners. However, there are very strict guidelines enforced by the IRS regarding who can and cannot be classified as an independent contractor, and huge penalties if those rules are not followed. According to IRS publication 15-A: "The general rule is that an individual is an independent contractor if you, the person for whom the services are performed, have the right to control or direct only the result of the work and not the means and methods of accomplishing the result." If you are unsure how to classify someone, you may file IRS Form SS-8 and the IRS will determine the work status.

Personnel Files

If you do choose to hire people, it is important to keep complete files to cover yourself legally. During the hiring process, the employee must complete a W-4 form to determine tax withholdings and an I-9 form to confirm U.S. citizenship. Copies of these should be included in the personnel file along with a completed job application, written job description, resume and references, and results of background and drug tests performed. In addition, you may consider having your employees sign an agreement stating that they will keep all company information confidential.

Setting Policies

Your business will run more smoothly if you establish clear, written policies for your employees to follow. A comprehensive handbook will assist with training new employees and may help prevent future problems or confusion regarding procedures and guidelines. Every employee should be required to sign a statement that they have read and understand the handbook. This form is then placed in the personnel file.

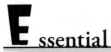

Having a company handbook to distribute to employees helps make your policy clear and irrefutable. The ideal is to avoid any gray areas as far as what is expected, as well as the consequences if the expectations are not met.

Your handbook may start out with the company history and mission statement. It should at least include policies on sexual harassment, discrimination, dress code, and drug use. As a personal-training business, you may also consider addressing the use of performance-enhancing drugs such as steroids, because a steroid scandal could put you out of business, or at least cost you a great deal of money. You might also consider including information on pay periods, benefits, performance reviews, and continuing education.

Be sure to include a policy against trainers becoming involved romantically with their clients. That type of situation could result in embarrassment at the least, and a lawsuit at the worst. You should also cover stealing money or products, giving away free sessions, or anything else that results in loss of profitability.

Chapter 9

Making Sure You Are Covered: Liability and Insurance

Being a personal trainer brings with it very serious considerations and risks. Due to the physical nature of the job, both trainers and clients have the potential to become injured. You can safeguard yourself, your business, and your future by understanding your legal responsibilities and obtaining proper insurance. You cannot predict or control the future. Anything could happen, and adequate preparation is your best protection against unforeseen circumstances.

Are You Liable?

Liability is a legal term for responsibility. When you are working with clients, you are responsible for their safety. This includes providing a safe work space, well-maintained equipment, and proper instruction and supervision. You can even be held liable for the advice you give. You need to protect yourself from litigation by educating yourself and your clients and by keeping proper records.

Scope of Practice

As a personal trainer, you have been trained to evaluate clients' fitness levels and create and implement exercise programs. It is your duty and responsibility to perform only the tasks for which you have been trained. If you are not also a certified athletic trainer or physician, and you are attempting to evaluate an injury, you are acting outside your scope of practice. This is also the case if you are not a licensed massage therapist and are massaging a client. Failing to stay within your scope of practice is irresponsible and can result in your causing harm to a client or being named in a lawsuit.

 **Alert**

A personal trainer can be found liable for making recommendations that result in a client becoming injured. This is especially true if you are receiving payment for endorsing the recommended product or service. If you choose to give advice outside your scope of practice, you need to make it clear that you are speaking only from personal experience or out of personal preference.

Standard of Care

Even though there are no laws specifically governing personal trainers, your actions must measure up to certain standards of professionalism. These standards are based on common practices within the industry. Whatever actions you take should be in line with accepted practices by other professionals.

If a personal trainer is sued, the court will base its decision on whether or not the actions in question measure up to the minimal standard and quality of care expected of a personal trainer. For example, if a trainer puts together a program for a client who then suffers an injury, the trainer will only be held liable if the program is inappropriate given the client's age and medical and exercise histories. The court would have to determine if other professionals with the same training would have acted in a similar manner given the same situation.

Negligence

If your actions or lack of action result in a client becoming injured, you could be found negligent by a court of law. Negligence typically occurs when a trainer fails to stay within her scope of practice or fails to uphold the standard of care for personal trainers. A trainer may be found negligent if a client sustains an injury because she failed to supervise him during a session, did not properly maintain the equipment, or recommended an unsafe exercise.

Protecting Yourself from Lawsuits

As unpleasant as the topic of lawsuits can be, it is a necessary topic for discussion. You need to do everything in your power to prevent being sued and to win a suit, should one be brought against you. Proper documentation, along with the development and use of informed consent and liability waivers, may help protect you from lawsuits. These forms must be able to hold up to scrutiny by a court of law and should be written or at least reviewed by a lawyer.

Informed Consent and Liability Waivers

The purpose of informed consent is to make the client aware of the dangers and risks of the activities he will be performing. By signing the form, the client acknowledges he is aware of and willing to accept the risks involved in participating in an exercise program. This is not the same thing as a waiver. A waiver will actually release you, the trainer, from responsibility for possible injury or death resulting from your programs. Neither of these forms will cover you if your behavior was grossly negligent, so always act with caution and care. Maintaining your standard of care and acting within your scope of practice are essential components to preventing lawsuits.

Proper Documentation

When you are working with a client, keep dated records of the exercises they performed and at what intensity. It is best to record the information during the session so you do not have to rely on your memory and do not have to worry about it later. You might also consider making a note of what you discussed during the appointment. While this is done partly to track a client's progress, it is also another form of protection against lawsuits. If the court questions your actions or advice, you have a written record of exactly what the client did during every session, as well as your recommendations to the client.

The Need for Insurance

Insurance is basically risk management. It protects you, your assets, and your business against situations that could cause you financial difficulties. There is insurance for just about everything these days:

automotive, fire, theft, and rain. You can even buy specialty insurance for personal watercraft and winter sports. Availability is certainly not a concern when you are shopping for insurance, but it can be difficult to know what types of insurance to buy.

Professional Liability

As a personal trainer, this type of insurance is a must. It will cover you and your employees in the event of injury due to:

- Inadequate supervision
- Inadequate instruction
- Equipment malfunction
- Improper use of equipment
- Sexual harassment

Even if you are insured through your employer, you should still obtain your own policy, especially if you do any training outside of the club. If you do not have this type of insurance, you could end up paying hundreds of thousands of dollars in court fees, legal fees, medical bills, lost wages, and pain and suffering. You may purchase this insurance and never need to use it. But if you are sued, even if the suit is unwarranted, and you do not have coverage, you will probably lose everything.

Medical

Medical insurance provides coverage against loss due to illness or injury. It pays for doctor appointments, prescriptions, hospital stays, trips to the emergency room, and some other health-related situations. This form of insurance is important because medical expenses can add up quickly. Prescriptions can cost hundreds of dollars per month, as can a visit to the doctor with blood work. A hospital stay can leave you with thousands of dollars in debt.

Each plan is unique in the deductibles, copays, and coverage offered. If you are employed by a health club as a full-time employee, you may be covered through their medical insurance policy. However, with the rise in medical costs, many health clubs are either not offering medical benefits or are requiring their employees to pay a portion of the cost. If you are an independent contractor or own your own business, medical insurance can be one of your biggest expenses. If you think you are healthy and do not need insurance, you are mistaken. One major illness or injury will leave you paying medical bills for a very long time.

E ssential

Before you purchase liability insurance, check to see if your legal fees will be covered. This can become a huge expense, even if a lawsuit does not make it to court. Lawyers charge a significant hourly rate, and you want to make sure you can afford the best when it comes to defending yourself in a court of law.

Disability

Disability insurance covers you in case you are unable to work for an extended period of time. The reason behind your injury or illness does not matter for coverage. This should not be confused with Worker's Comp insurance. With disability insurance, you will receive benefits even when the problem is not work related. If you are an employee, find out if your employer pays for your disability insurance. Most of the time, purchasing this form of insurance will be your responsibility. If you are self-employed, this is a must. Again, even the healthiest individuals can end up unable to work due to accident or illness.

Business Insurance Plan (BOP)

BOPs are insurance packages for small businesses. They simplify life by offering a combination of insurances so all major property and liability is in one package: property insurance, business interruption insurance, and general liability. You will only need this type of insurance if you lease or own the building you work in. Notice that professional liability is not included in a BOP and must be purchased separately.

Where to Find Insurance

Finding a company to insure you is never a problem. There are insurance agencies on every corner. However, as a personal trainer, you will require special considerations. You will be best served by an agent or agency that is familiar with the ins and outs of the fitness industry.

Certifying Organization

One of the advantages of becoming certified is that the organization that certified you will likely offer professional liability insurance. You can usually purchase a significant amount of coverage for a very reasonable price. Familiarize yourself with the policy and make sure it provides coverage that you are comfortable with. If the coverage is insufficient, there are many other ways to obtain coverage.

 Fact

There are plenty of insurance companies who specialize in covering personal trainers. IHRSA has a search engine called buyer smart where you can find some of these companies. To perform a search, log on to *www.ihrsa.org/buyersmart*. Or you can try *www.trainerinsurance .com*, *www.sportsfitness.com,* or *www.kandkinsurance.com*.

Insurance Agencies

Insurance agencies deal with many different insurance companies and may be able to find you the best coverage at the cheapest price. If you open the yellow pages, you will find any number of insurance agencies. After some investigation, you will likely find that many of those agencies do not understand the health and fitness industry. Your best bet may be to network with other trainers to see what agency they use.

Purchasing Insurance

Insurance can be one of your biggest expenses. While it is a necessity, make sure you do not pay for insurance you do not need; more is not always better. The more coverage you have, the more it will cost you. If you are running your own business, you want to keep your overhead low. If your expenses go up, you will have to pass on that cost to your clients by increasing your rates. Do not get oversold on insurance. Purchase only what you need.

Alert

Keep good records of your policies and the payments you make. In the event that you need to file a claim, this information should be at your fingertips. If you have an insurance agent, they should also have copies, but don't count on it. Proper record keeping will allow you to file a claim and recover damages more easily.

As a consumer, you want the biggest and best bang for your buck. Before signing on the dotted line, obtain at least three bids from various sources. You might consider requesting bids from companies that specialize in insuring personal trainers and from some local agents. Compare the coverage they provide with the fees you will pay and find the best deal.

Reassessing Your Insurance Needs

Reassess what you need for coverage annually. As your business grows, so may your need for more or different coverage. Did you hire any employees? Move your business location? Acquire new equipment? Any of these factors may influence the type and amount of coverage you may need. Assessing your insurance needs annually may also help to defray costs from insurance you do not need. Reviewing your policy prior to the renewal date can ensure that you will be properly insured. Before you commit to another year, you might consider obtaining bids again to see if you can find a better deal.

Insuring Your Employees

If you are fortunate enough to employ other trainers, then you will need to make sure they are covered under your professional liability insurance policy. Your employees are providing services and products under your company name. Therefore, you are liable for their actions. You need to protect both the clients and trainers by providing adequate coverage. If the actions of you or one of your employees results in injury to a client, your policy will ensure that he will be adequately compensated.

Worker's Compensation Insurance

The government requires that you carry Worker's Comp insurance for all employees. This type of insurance covers your employees for injuries sustained on the job. If the government finds you are not carrying this insurance or not carrying the right amount, you will be assessed a hefty fine. The amount you will pay is based on a number of factors, including your employees' job descriptions and the work they perform. It will also depend on your company's history of claims. If the company's claims are low, meaning few if any accidents have been reported, the worker's compensation rate will be low. The greater the number of claims that are filed, the higher the insurance rate will be.

Medical

Paying your employees' medical expenses is not required by law. However, you will increase employee satisfaction by offering this benefit. You will also be more likely to keep your employees for longer periods of time. If you cannot afford to insure everyone, consider insuring one or two key employees. If they are that important to your business, they are worth spending a little money to keep them around. Another option is having your employees pay a portion of their own insurance. Again, this is not a requirement, but is certainly a nice perk.

Chapter 10

Establishing Policies for an Effective Business

In order to run an effective business, you must create an infrastructure for your company to stand on. You need to have policies and procedures addressing all aspects of your business, from scheduling appointments to collecting payments. Putting these policies in writing will make clear to your clients what they can expect and what is expected of them. This can help avoid unpleasant situations and may ultimately protect you and your business from litigation.

Open for Business: Scheduling Your Week

Are you becoming a personal trainer for a career, or just looking for some part-time income? Knowing how much money you need and how many hours you are able to train will effectively dictate your client load. Your schedule will also be influenced by how many clients have purchased training sessions. The exception to all of this will be those employed by a health club or gym. As an employee, you may have little say about the hours you work.

Setting Your Hours

You are your business, and need to treat yourself as such. All businesses have hours of operation, and it is important to establish these hours and stick by them. Make it clear to your clients that while you can be somewhat flexible, you are also not at their beck and call. Most likely they have jobs, and must be present during certain hours. In the same way, they need to respect your hours of operation.

The great thing about personal training is that you can make it work around your lifestyle. If you need to be home to see your kids off to school, you can start training at 9 A.M. If you do not like working weekends, you can work Monday–Friday. This flexibility is a blessing, but can become a curse. If you do not hold to your predetermined working hours, sooner or later there will be no cohesiveness to your work schedule. You may find yourself working odd hours, or working day and night with no time left for family or recreation.

E ssential

Whether you are traveling to your clients or working in a facility, you need to establish set operating hours. This will create boundaries for yourself and your clients so you do not end up working more hours than you want to. You may be surprised by some of the demands and requests your clients will make if you allow them.

Your clients' priority is fitting in his workout, as it should be. It is up to you to be concerned with your own schedule. Clients will ask all kinds of things of you. They may want to workout at 5 A.M., 10 P.M., or on Sunday. This may be fine with you, or it may be a burden. Setting your hours and giving them to your clients in writing will make it easier to say no when you need to.

Making Appointments

Having standard operating procedures for setting and completing your first appointments will simplify your life and decrease mistakes. By asking the same questions and following the same procedures with all of your clients, you will form good habits and your practices will become routine.

Before you set an appointment with a new client, obtain some background information to make sure you can handle what she needs. Ask about her age, health, fitness level, exercise history, and what she wants to accomplish by working with you. You do not need to get into too much detail. Just get a general idea of where she is coming from and where she wishes to go. If you feel you can help her, set the appointment and give or mail her a new client packet. This packet should contain:

- A bio of you and your company
- Informed consent form
- Liability waiver
- Health questionnaire
- Lifestyle information form
- Frequently asked questions
- Payment and cancellation policies
- Billing information
- Medical release form

Request that before she meets with you, she completes the health and lifestyle questionnaires so you do not have to spend valuable time completing paperwork. Make it clear that your first appointment will consist mainly of exchanging information and evaluating her fitness level. Instruct the client to wear loose-fitting comfortable clothes and sneakers, and to bring a water bottle.

Alert

If you start taking the attitude of "I'm already here so what's another hour," that extra hour can turn into two or three more hours, and soon you will be putting in nine- or ten-hour days. Working this type of schedule is a sure way to end up tired and burned out.

Planning for Your Financial Needs

Finances will play a major role in the number of hours you choose to work. Everyone has a certain standard of living to which they are accustomed or to which they aspire. What is yours? Figure out how much money you need to live and divide it by what you charge per hour. That will provide you with an idea of how many appointments you will need every month. Give yourself a cushion for the times when you are slow, have cancellations, or cannot work for some reason. You may also want to leave a few hours open each week so you can reschedule or move clients around if necessary. This will limit lost revenue due to cancellations.

Policies for Accidents and Emergencies

For your own protection and the welfare of your clients, you should have a written plan in place to deal with accidents and emergencies. You are working with people in a physical manner, and inevitably things will go wrong. People will fall off treadmills and trip over equipment. Most of the time there are no resulting injuries, but you must be prepared for the worst. If you are well prepared, you will increase the chances that there will be a favorable outcome.

Your Emergency Action Plan

An emergency action plan (EAP) is just what it sounds like—a plan that you implement in the event of an emergency. If you are working in a club, they will likely have their own plan with which you should be familiar. If this is not the case, encourage management to create a plan.

If you are working independently or in your clients' homes, there will be several key components to your EAP. First, always carry a copy of your clients' health forms with you. If for some reason an individual loses consciousness, you should be able to provide the EMTs with their health history information. You will also be able to call the emergency contact person they listed to make them aware of the situation. Keep your cell phone with you at all times, or be sure you have access to a land line in case you need to call 911. You should be able to provide the dispatcher with the exact address of your location as well as which entrance to the building the EMTs should use. This could save valuable time if the person is in cardiac arrest. You should at a minimum be trained in CPR and First Aid, so handle the situation as you were trained, but stay within your scope of practice. If you have employees, put your EAP in writing and periodically review the procedures to keep them fresh in everyone's minds.

Creating an Accident Report Form

The purpose of an accident report form is to document any mishaps resulting in injuries to your client. It's important to have an accurate description of what transpired, especially in the event of a lawsuit. When an incident occurs, manage it according to your emergency action plan. As soon as the situation is under control, fill out the entire accident report form. Ideally, the injured party will be well enough to sign the form, indicating their agreement with what you have written. In some cases, however, a person may refuse to sign the document or may not be able to. If this occurs, obtain the signature of a witness, preferably a neutral party.

 Question

How Can I Become Certified in CPR and First Aid?
Find your local chapter of the American Red Cross at *www.redcross. org* or American Heart Association at *www.americanheart.org*. They provide classes where you can learn and become certified in first aid and CPR. Remember that you will also have to keep your certifications current by taking a recertification class every two to three years.

The accident report form should always contain the following information:

- Name of the injured party
- Date and time of the injury
- Location of the accident
- Sequence of events, in detail
- Steps taken following the incident (called 911, administered first aid)
- Signature of the person filling out the report
- Signature of injured party and witnesses

Document this information as soon as possible, so the incident is fresh in your mind.

Even if you think the incident was minor, fill out the report. You never know when that little bump on the head will actually be a concussion, or when a client's twisted ankle will really be an avulsion fracture. People who hurt themselves may be embarrassed to admit the severity of the injury, especially if they are surrounded by people. You may not find out until later that the incident was not minor at all.

Payment and Billing Policies

Requesting payment and dealing with money is certainly not the most enjoyable part of personal training. However, the fact is you are in business and you need to make money. You are providing a service for which you must be paid. To avoid any misunderstanding, be upfront and clear about what you expect from your clients in the areas of pricing, form of payment, and time of payment.

Collecting Fees

There are several ways you may collect your fees. It is common for trainers to require payment upon completion of the session. However, some clients like to pay up-front, while others prefer to be billed. Some trainers will allow clients to choose when and how they want to pay, while others have a strict policy regarding when the session is paid and the means of payment.

Invoicing can be a nice option for clients who train with you multiple times per week. Instead of writing twelve checks per month, you can bill them monthly, which requires them to write only one check. If you do choose to send invoices to your clients, you may create your own or use any number of programs available for small businesses. Your decision will likely depend on how many invoices you will be sending monthly. At a minimum, the following information should be included on the invoice:

- Name of your business
- Address to which the payment should be sent
- Client's name
- Date of invoice
- The number of sessions for which payment is due

- Total amount due
- Date by when the payment must be received

If you do not mind waiting for payment, clients who see you multiple times per week may appreciate this method of payment; it simplifies their lives. Keep in mind, however, that your bill will be one of many and may not be as high of a priority, so payment could take longer.

If you collect money after each session, you will always have a cash flow. You will not have to concern yourself with budgeting receivables. Asking clients to pay by the session will also reduce the sticker shock. Some people find it easier to pay $50 per session for ten sessions than to receive a bill for $500 at the end of the month.

There will be clients who wish to pay for multiple sessions up-front. They will likely be looking for a discounted rate. This is a common practice in the industry, and it too has pros and cons. The benefit of selling packages is that you have the money up-front; you are guaranteed those appointments. If someone misses an appointment, they have already paid for it, and you do not have to chase them down for payment. The drawback is that if you discount your services too much, it cheapens the perceived value. You may also end up spending the money before you complete the sessions you were paid for. Then it feels like you are working for free.

Essential

If you do choose to sell packages, be specific about the timeframe in which your clients may use the sessions, and whether or not the sessions are transferable to someone else. Be as flexible as possible for your customers without causing your business to lose money.

Forms of Payment

There are four different ways you can accept payment from your clients. Most trainers who work on their own accept only cash and checks. Those who work in or own a facility may also accept debit and credit card payments. There are benefits and drawbacks to all forms of payment. Figure out what best suits your business and set your policies accordingly.

Some clients will prefer to use credit cards over cash or checks, especially if the amount owed is a large sum. Credit cards are convenient and many people use them for the rewards programs offered by the credit card companies. People will be more willing to make big purchases if you offer this option of payment. If you choose to do so, you will first have to be approved by a financial institution. You will also be charged a fee by the credit card processing company. If you are an independent trainer, you must determine whether the benefit outweighs the cost for this option.

Electronic Funds Transfer (EFT) will take money directly from the client's checking account. This form of payment is only necessary if you own a facility and are charging a membership fee. You will be required to pay for this service as well.

Checks offer an easy way to accept payment. Many people feel comfortable with checks because they are not carrying around large amounts of cash. You may at times find an account with insufficient funds to cover the check you cashed. You will then be charged a fee by the bank. When you write your payment policy, include that you will charge a fee for this situation. You have to deal with the inconvenience, as well as the penalty imposed upon you. It is well within your legal right to do so.

Accepting cash is the easiest way to conduct business. You have immediate access to your money, and you do not have to pay a handling fee, wait for a check to clear, or deal with insufficient funds. As the saying goes, cash is king. The danger with cash is, if it is in your hands, you will be more tempted to spend it.

Refunds

Having a refund policy will put people at ease about buying your products or services. Basically, you want to let your clients know they will be 100 percent satisfied, or receive their money back. You will also have to consider your policy on refunding packages if you sell them. You may choose to refund a percentage of the purchase price or all of it, depending on circumstances. At the end of the day, keep your client satisfied. Losing a long-term customer over a refund is like cutting off your nose to spite your face.

Handling Lateness

You and your clients lead very busy lives. Inevitably, there will be times when one of you is late for your appointment. You have to handle these situations in a way that is comfortable for you and fair to both you and your clients. Whatever you decide, put your policy in writing and discuss it with your clients. You may even consider writing it in the form of a contract, describing the responsibilities of both client and trainer.

Alert

It is easy to confuse being taken advantage of with providing good customer service. In a misguided effort to keep clients happy, trainers can become overly accommodating. If you understand and behave as though your time is valuable, your clients will also. If, on the other hand, you sacrifice your schedule too much, your clients will not respect your time.

When the Client Is Late

While your clients may make every effort to arrive at their appointments on time, there will be times where they arrive late. If this is a rare occurrence and you have the time to do so, you may choose to allow your client to stay beyond the scheduled hour and finish the workout. This is an example of going the extra mile to provide good customer service. However, by doing so you are going into the next time slot. If you have someone scheduled for that time, you will simply need to complete as much of the workout as possible in whatever time remains. Keep in mind that you do not want this occurrence to become a habit. If a client is chronically late, make it clear that her scheduled time is for a specific hour and does not begin when she arrives for the appointment. If your client schedules an appointment for 10 A.M., she is paying you for your service from 10–11 A.M. You may not have a client at 11 A.M., but you will likely have something else you need or want to do at that time.

When the Trainer Is Late

If you know you will not be on time for an appointment, contact your client to let him know you will be late. Try to give an approximate time for your arrival. Your clients' time is just as valuable as your own, and you should respect their time as much as you expect them to respect yours. You also need to be accountable for your lateness. Ask your client if they still want to keep the appointment or reschedule for a more convenient time.

If you and your client both have the time to extend the appointment, this is the simplest solution. If you are more than fifteen minutes late and the client is unable to make up the time, either do not charge for the appointment or offer a discounted rate. If you have really put your client out, you might consider offering him a free session. Your ultimate goal is customer satisfaction, so you need to do what it takes to rectify the situation in a satisfactory manner.

Missed Appointments and Cancellations

Your business is your livelihood, and if clients are constantly canceling and missing appointments, you will lose money. Establishing written policies to address these issues will minimize lost revenue. The document should be worded in a clear and concise manner so there is no room for confusion or argument.

Writing Your Cancellation Policy

Your cancellation policy will make your clients accountable for missed workouts. The reason behind this policy is, that given enough notice, you may be able to fill the appointment time with another client. There is a fee charged to the client if he cancels after the allotted time. Some trainers charge a percentage of the session, while others require the full amount of the session. You are a professional and your time is valuable. If people miss appointments with their doctors, dentists, or therapists, they are charged a fee. You live by your appointments just as they do, and deserve a similar respect for your valuable time.

E ssential

All of your policies should be written clearly and specifically. Make every attempt to address all possible scenarios. You can always relax a policy to make allowances for a special circumstance, but you cannot go back and make your policies more stringent.

Your written policy should contain a standard time frame during which the client can cancel without penalty. The exact period of time is up to your discretion, but is typically between twelve and forty-eight hours. Some trainers will include a clause stating that if the client reschedules for another time in the same week, the fee will be waived. This will depend, of course, on the availability of the trainer. Once you have discussed this policy with your client and feel confident she understands it, request her signature to demonstrate her agreement, then give her a copy for her records.

Handling No-Shows

Your cancellation policy should also address no-shows. Every so often you will have a client fail to show up for an appointment and not call to cancel or explain. This can be a frustrating and disconcerting occurrence. Before you lose your temper, remember that there may have been an emergency, sickness, or schedule mix-up. There is also a chance your client is simply running late, so give him ten or fifteen minutes to get there. If your client still has not arrived, try calling to find out what happened. If he simply forgot, you must decide whether to charge him or reschedule the appointment. If you are unable to reach the client, leave a message explaining the missed appointment and ask him to call you at his earliest convenience. Remember, you do not know the reason for the no-show, so avoid addressing compensation in a voice mail.

You do not want to lose a client over one no-show, so be careful not to get too pushy about payment. For most people, this will be a total accident and it will not be repeated. They will realize their mistake and understand that you have only a limited amount of time to work. However, if this becomes a chronic occurrence with a client, you either need to charge them for missed appointments or tell them you can no longer work with them.

Chapter 11

Marketing Your Business

A quality marketing plan is the key to making your business a success. It will help you determine if there is a need for your services, give you the information you need to set competitive prices, and help you convince people to pay for your services. A marketing plan consists of market research, identifying a target group, identifying and assessing the competition, defining the service you are selling, pricing, advertising, and promotion. The more comprehensive you make your plan, the better your chances for success.

Marketing Your Products and Services

Before beginning a marketing campaign, you must do quite of bit of legwork. Without the proper information, you will have no purpose or direction and will be wasting time, energy, and money. Start by determining the level of demand for your products and services, and identifying the customers who will likely purchase them. You should also know and understand the businesses that are competing for this same group of customers. Armed with this information, you will be able to move in the right direction, instead of operating blindly or without purpose.

Know Your Customers

It is unwise and wasteful to advertise to an unspecified audience. You should have a clear definition, in writing, of who you are marketing to and how you will go about marketing to this targeted group. While it would be nice if everyone wanted to utilize your services,

the fact is most can't or won't. There will be a relatively small population of those with the desire and financial capacity to hire you or join
your club. The more specific you can be about who they are, the less
money you will need to spend on marketing.

Fact

Performing market research can save significant time and money
in the long run. Market research involves identifying and gathering
information about your current and potential customers, your competitors, and the fitness market. It helps determine what your customers want and need, and how you can provide it.

Defining Your Customers

Defining who your potential customers are will help sort out your
advertising needs and give you direction. You can identify them by
describing your niche. Who do you want your services to target? If, for
example, you plan on working with post-rehab patients, you will focus
your advertising efforts on orthopedic surgeons and physical therapists. If you spend your time marketing to the local chess club, you will
be wasting your time and money. The best advertising campaign will
yield disappointing results if the wrong group of people is targeted.

Identifying Strengths and Weaknesses of
the Competition

Are you offering your customers something different from what
the competition offers? If the answer is yes, your job is easy. You will
have the new service that no one else has, and you can corner the
market. If the answer is no, you must define what makes your services
better than the competition. What sets you apart? Start by answering
the following questions:

- How many competitors are in your area?
- What products and services do they provide?

- What is their price point?
- What type of advertising do they use?
- How long have they been in business?
- Do they control a large portion of the market?

Find out as much information as you can, in the greatest detail possible. If they have been in business longer than you, learn from their successes and failures. Obtaining this information will save you time and money. In addition, the more intimately you know and understand your competition, the easier it will be to make your services stand out.

Objectives and Goals

Goals and objectives will give you a direction and help you plan your course of action. They will also help you measure the level or lack of success of your marketing and advertising campaign. Just as you do with clients, break your objectives down into long- and short-term goals. Long-term objectives pertaining to marketing usually involve financial achievements such as an increase in revenue or profits, hiring more staff, or expanding the business in some way. Once you have some written objectives, you can start breaking them down into goals. Goals should be written and specific. Make them as detailed as possible and include time frames. If the long-term goal is to increase memberships by 10 percent over the next year, the short-term advertising goals for the first month might look like this:

- Book one speaking engagement at a local event
- Volunteer at one local event
- Create and place an ad in the local paper
- Print and distribute 500 promotional flyers
- Start creating a Web site for the business

Advertising to Your Market

Advertising is a great marketing tool. It allows you to promote your business through public communication. The goal of advertising is to develop innovative methods to persuade new customers to purchase your services, and old customers to increase or expand their utilization of your services.

What Are You Trying to Achieve?

In order for your advertising to send the right message to your potential customers, you must have clearly defined goals and objectives. What exactly are you trying to accomplish with your advertising campaign? If you are promoting sports-specific programs, your objective is to reach high school athletes. Your goal is to have them sign up for your sports-specific training packages. You now know the market you're going after (high school athletes), and where they are located (at the high school). Now, how do you make students and their parents aware of and willing to pay for your services? You could advertise at the games or run a promotion at a local restaurant often frequented after games. Your options are only limited by your creativity. The most important factor is being clear with your objectives.

The ultimate goal of advertising is creating more business. Every ad you place is a result of the desire to increase profits. You want to persuade potential customers to buy your services because your company is better than the competition. Whatever you do, do not lie about or embellish what you are offering. This will create a negative reputation and lead to loss of business. Do, however, be as creative as possible. The more creative your ads and your approach, the more you will be noticed.

Reaching Your Market or Niche

The goal in advertising for small business is not to reach as many people as possible. Instead, it is to reach and connect with your target market in the least-expensive way possible. The more information you can gather about your target market, the more successfully you will achieve this result. As a personal trainer or the owner of a studio, you will be dealing with many different people. Examine the current demographics of your clientele. Consider gender; occupation; age; the number of times per week they work with a trainer; what other services they purchase from you; the times of day they exercise; how long they have been with you; etc. This information will help you narrow your focus.

Once you have a specific idea of who you are marketing to, create the advertising campaign around that group of people. If, for example, you find that most of your business comes from housewives who range in age from thirty to forty-five, then that is where you want to focus your advertising efforts. Ask some of your clients where they shop and what publications they read. Consider placing ads in the most common ones. Find out what local businesses they frequent and post flyers or leave business cards at those locations. If they spend a great deal of time in the car, radio ads may be the way to go. Putting the time into researching your market will enable you to create a campaign that will yield positive results.

E ssential

Remember, advertising costs money, and you want to receive the biggest possible return on your investment. You can only influence buying behavior if you know precisely who you are targeting and what they really want.

Types of Advertising Media

Every successful business uses some form of advertising. It creates an avenue for companies to be in contact with current and potential customers. The old adage is true; out of sight, out of mind. You have to constantly keep your name and image in front of people or they will forget you. Advances in technology have made advertising much easier and more cost–effective. It can still be quite expensive, however, so you must determine what form will work best while fitting into your budget.

Word of Mouth

Stop for a minute and think about your doctor, dentist, insurance agent, mechanic, hair stylist, and anyone else who provides you with a service. Most likely you did not thumb through the yellow pages or newspaper classifieds to find these people. You probably asked a trusted friend or relative who they used and if they were happy with them. You may not have even had to ask. Most people who are happy with the service they received will talk about it. For this reason, word of mouth is the best form of advertising, and it costs nothing. It is only effective, however, if you are providing top-notch service to your customers.

Question

How can I capitalize on word of mouth advertising?
Be prepared. Give your clients brochures and business cards to distribute to their friends and families. Emphasize how much you appreciate and rely on referrals. You can even develop a referral system where you offer discounted training sessions or other incentives for existing customers who refer a new customer.

Flyers, Brochures, and Business Cards

Flyers, brochures, and business cards are relatively inexpensive to make. The simplest method is to buy them online or have them designed by a professional. If you are computer savvy, you may choose to make them yourself using special software. You can then visit your local office supply store or professional printer and make copies. Printing at home is not time- or cost-effective when dealing with large quantities. Professional printers buy their paper in bulk and offer a variety of colors and paper quality. Their printers are made to generate large quantities in a short period of time. Your home office printer will be slow and use a great deal of ink.

Now that you have this print medium, what do you do with them? This is where it becomes important to know your market. If you know who your potential customers are, and the places they frequent, it is much easier to get your information in their hands. Suppose you are going after the sports-performance market. You may obtain permission to hand out flyers or brochures at the entrance to games at the local high school. Make an appointment with the school's athletic director and ask for a copy of the coach's mailing list. If this is not possible, perhaps he will allow you to place information in their school mailboxes. The only expense you have incurred is the printing of the information and your time. This is still less expensive than running an ad in the newspaper, and you are getting face-to-face contact with people and building relationships.

The Internet

Imagine; your business can be seen by millions of people with just a touch of the finger. The Internet has rapidly become a media juggernaut—it seems everyone these days has a Web site or blog. It also means your business can get lost in the World Wide Web.

A Web site is a valuable advertising medium for your business. The cost for hosting a Web site is minimal compared to running radio or television ads. But what is the best way to attract customers to your Web site? By including your Web address on anything with your company name: flyers, brochures, business cards, print ads, etc. This also increases the level of professionalism portrayed by your business.

Alert

If you do not want to look like a second-rate business, refrain from placing your advertisements on the windshields of people's cars. People get annoyed and rarely pay attention to this form of advertising. The practice is not wise for a professional establishment.

Your Web site may contain all of the services and products you offer to your customers. You can include pictures of your facility, weekly newsletters, helpful tips for your members, and more. Your Web site is also a great place to develop your warm market. People who visit the site may contact you for more information, or you can put a request on your site that people provide their name and e-mail address. Once you have a potential client's contact information, you can generate a warm call. Another nice feature is that you can easily track how many visitors have accessed the site.

The Internet is also a great place to perform research on your competitors. Examine the type of information contained on their sites and the products and services they offer. How do they drive people to their sites? Again, look at the positives and negatives, successes and failures, and learn from them. If they are doing something that works, do it. If they are doing something that isn't working, do not waste your time.

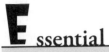

Essential

If you do not have the knowledge to create a Web site for your business or the funds to hire someone, you might consider bartering for services. There are many people who are skilled in Web design. Find someone who is interested in training with you and work out a deal. This can be a win-win situation.

Newspaper and Magazine Ads

Have you ever noticed how many advertisements appear in newspapers and magazines? They are located on every page because an extraordinary number of people read them on a daily basis. Circulations for newspapers and magazines can be in the thousands, even the hundreds of thousands, and many of these people pay attention to the ads. If you choose to place an ad in one of these mediums, how many people reading them would be part of your target audience? The wise choice for small businesses is to advertise as locally as possible. Town newspapers or other local publications are generally worthwhile investments. The cost of placing an ad is lower, and a higher percentage of their readers fall within the targeted population.

If you are interested in pursuing or investigating this option, contact the ad representative at the publication of your choice to request a media package. These packages may contain demographics on their readers, the prices of advertising, and a description of the publication. When making your final decision, take the following into consideration:

- How much will the ad cost?
- Where will the ad be placed within the publication?
- How many people will it reach?
- How many times will it reach them?
- What do you hope to accomplish with the ad?

The cost of the ad will depend on where it is placed. Ads located in the front or back are more expensive because they are more noticeable. The ads placed in the middle are cheaper but may be easily missed. You have to measure the cost versus benefit when deciding where to place the ad.

 Fact

Many publications will offer cheaper rates the longer you run the ad. Running an ad for a longer period of time can end up being more cost effective, because more customers will have the opportunity to read it.

Broadcast Media

Broadcast media includes radio and television. The purpose of this form of advertising is to sell people on the value of your services in a fifteen to thirty second time slot. If you are considering this type of advertising, know that your expenses will be two-fold. You will likely need to employ the services of a professional advertising agency to create the ad, and you will then pay the broadcasting company to run it.

Radio spots are less expensive than television, but still more expensive than print ads. Since your customers will not visually experience the ad, you must appeal to their other senses. A well-created ad can leave a great impression, while a poorly made ad may go completely unnoticed.

Contact sales representatives at your local radio stations to see what type of media packages they offer. Ask about their programming.

Do they have any health, fitness, or other programs related to wellness during which you could run your ad? This is not essential, but may help pinpoint your target audience. The station may also offer sponsorship advertising, where your company can sponsor the traffic report or the news. Ideally, you will be able to develop a package that is cost-effective for your company and will generate a significant amount of new business.

E ssential

Just because you cannot afford a full-page ad in your local newspaper doesn't mean your advertisement will not be effective. Small ads can be just as effective in reaching your target audience as large ones, especially if they are eye-catching.

Television is a highly effective way to send a message to the masses. Almost every household in the United States has a television, and while you do not need your commercial broadcast across the country, covering the local area can be beneficial. The cost of television ads can be extremely expensive, depending on your needs. Large companies use television as their main source of advertising because it creates brand recognition and image while reaching millions of people. Your needs are not this vast. Reaching thousands of people locally will be more than adequate for a small business.

If you are interested in placing a television ad, start by contacting sales representatives at your local stations or cable companies. Inquire about the types of services and packages they offer small businesses. Pricing will depend on:

- The length of the ad
- How many spots you buy
- The time of day the commercial airs
- The channel or channels on which it will appear
- The size of the market you wish to reach

The benefit of radio and television is that they capture your audience's attention. However, broadcast media can be risky and expensive for small businesses. People hear and see dozens of commercials, so yours will need to be especially creative in order to be noticed.

Examine your budget to see if and where this type of advertising fits in. You could end up using most or all of your advertising budget on this one area, and it may not provide you with an adequate return on your investment. There are many other cost-effective ways to reach your target audience.

Advertising and Your Budget

Advertising is a necessary expense. You will have limited success in your business if people are unaware of who you are and what services you offer. It is possible, however, to advertise without breaking the bank. While many modes of advertising cost money, there are ways to make it more cost-effective. Your first step is to determine how much advertising you need. Identify what you can afford to spend and create a budget and plan that fit your financial needs.

Alert

Don't forget to consider the cost of producing the commercial. Will you do it yourself, use a professional advertising company, or can the station produce the ad? These costs may be extensive and will need to be included in your budget.

Stay Within Your Budget

Your advertising budget will usually come from a percentage of your gross company income. If you find you have limited funds to put toward advertising, you will need to locate or create low-cost mediums that put your company in front of many consumers at one time. If you have a substantial budget you need not be concerned, but this is rarely the case for entrepreneurs and small business people. Play it smart and do only what you can afford—there is a point where cost outweighs benefit.

Free or Low-Cost Advertising

Most likely, if you own a studio or small personal-training business, your advertising budget will be small. You may have little or no funds to allot to advertising. But even with the smallest budget, there are ways to get your message out to your target audience; you simply have to work a little harder. With some effort and planning, you can be your own ad agent and make your business visible and appealing to the public.

The least-expensive form of advertising is word of mouth. The only drawback is you also have little or no control of the messages being relayed. Strategically placed flyers cost pennies and can generate business and name recognition. Post them in areas frequented by potential customers. E-mail communication is also free, but it is up to you to obtain addresses for a mailing list. You can send out weekly or monthly e-mails to your current and potential customers to keep your business visible.

Local newspapers typically offer a small space for press releases. These spots are offered at little or no cost and are a great way to announce to the public that you have a new product or service, a new location, new employee, or a special promotion.

If you have the interest and ability, you could offer to write articles pertaining to health and fitness, or even an advice column at no cost to the paper. In return, they may grant you some advertising space or put information about your business at the end of your article. You may not be getting paid, but having the free advertising and public relations is worth more than monetary compensation.

Promoting Yourself and Your Business

Promoting is simply one aspect of marketing. It keeps the products and services you offer in the minds of your customers. The goal of promoting is to increase demand for your services. Promoting is comprised of four parts: advertising, personal sales, sales promotions, and public relations.

Consumer Sales Promotions and Promotional Products

Sales promotions are marketing techniques used for a limited amount of time to increase customer demand. You may use them to promote your business, open a new location, announce a new product or service, or mark an anniversary. Sales promotions include: contests, coupons, loyalty rewards programs, free samples, and free products. They generate attention and excitement from your target market. One of the most popular promotions with health clubs are contests where the member who refers the most new members within a certain time period receives a bike, TV, or other large prize. A promotion does not have to be this big or expensive. You can make it as simple as giving out flyers with coupons for 10 percent off a training session. People love to get things for free or at a discount.

E ssential

Think about some of the T-shirts in your drawers. A good portion of them probably bear someone's company name, logo, or slogan. When you wear those shirts, you are a walking, free advertisement for the companies. In the same way, you can have your clients advertising for you. Just like Nike, you are creating name recognition. *Just Do It!*

A promotional product is any item bearing your company name or logo that you give to clients and potential clients. They are another way to advertise without spending a great deal of money. The use of promotional products is only limited to your imagination. Be sure to give people products they will use, so others will see them. Look around the gym and you'll notice that the majority of people are wearing T-shirts and carrying water bottles, making these two great promotional products for personal-training businesses.

Creating a Press Kit

A press kit contains information pertaining to you and your business. The purpose is to give potential customers and people who may refer customers in-depth knowledge of who you are and what you do. The design and contents of your press kit will say a great deal about you and can help you stand out from the crowd. The folder should look professional and be eye-catching, with your company's name and logo on the front. At a minimum, it should contain one or more business cards, a personal letter from you explaining your mission statement and the services you provide, and any relevant brochures or flyers. You may also include short bios on yourself and your employees. Promotional items are a nice addition as well—people love discounts and coupons.

Using Professional Advertising Agencies

You are not a professional advertising representative or design artist, you are a professional trainer. While you might be capable of creating an advertising campaign for your company, a professional would likely be better equipped and more effective. Therefore, if your budget allows you to use a professional agency, then do so. Ad agencies will do all of the legwork for you. They are accustomed to dealing with many types of businesses and various budgets. If you shop around, you may find an agency that is willing and able to work with what you need and can afford.

Finding the Right Agency

When looking for an ad agency, take into consideration that you are a small business. Obtaining referrals from other small business owners who have had positive experiences can save you both time and money. You don't want to end up with an agency where you will get lost among bigger fish. Find an agency where you will receive the care and attention you deserve.

Conducting interviews is a helpful way to see if the recommended agency or agencies can meet your needs. When you interview potential agencies, bring along a list of your goals and objectives. You can also bring your mission statement or even your entire business plan.

The more information you provide, the better the agent will understand you and your company. Some agencies specialize in specific fields and professions, so make sure the one you choose is capable of helping you meet your objectives and goals. If you find a small agency or an independent contractor, you may be able to negotiate rates and fees or even barter for services.

How Ad Agencies Work for You

Ad agencies provide many services. They can develop your whole campaign from start to finish, or simply design an ad. You may want them to act as consultants and tell you where to focus your efforts, but then do the rest of the work yourself. Doing some of the work yourself will help keep down costs. Through careful discussion and consideration, determine what you are capable of, comfortable with, and what you can afford.

Measuring the Effectiveness of Advertising

Most likely you will evaluate and test your clients at the beginning of their exercise programs. You will then periodically retest them to see if the program is effective. You should approach your advertisements the same way, to make sure they are cost-effective and resulting in new business. If you are using an ad agency, they should have a method to analyze ad placement and response. The last thing you want to be doing is spending money on ads that are not attracting customers.

Tracking advertisements is crucial to small businesses. When placing an advertisement, you can code it and request that new customers bring it with them when they come. Also, when a new client contacts you, ask them how they heard about the business. Was it by word of mouth, a newspaper ad, brochures in a doctor's office, online, or some other way? Keep track of the responses so you can see what generates the most business. You can then focus your efforts more effectively.

Chapter 12

Networking

Networking is an inexpensive and quite profitable way to grow your business. Unlike marketing and advertising, you do not have to pay to network. You are simply meeting and getting to know people. It is about giving and receiving favors, but has more to do with connecting with people than selling your services. The beauty of networking is that it can be done anytime, anywhere. You can network with every person you come in contact with during the course of your day. The more people you interact with, the better your results.

Networking Basics

The purpose of networking is to connect with people who need your services or those who can give you referrals. This may mean meeting with other professionals to discuss how you can work together to increase business. But it can also mean talking to the person in front of you in the line at the grocery store. People who excel at networking exchange information, resources, and support; and most importantly, they set goals.

Ask Questions Then Listen and Observe

There is one way to find out if a person you meet is someone with whom you want to have a networking relationship—ask questions. Ask them about their jobs, what they do, and how they like it. People love to talk about themselves and will likely be eager to answer. Really listen to their answers, but let them talk. Show genuine interest in the topic of discussion, and be yourself. People can spot a phony a mile away, and it will turn them off. These questions help you obtain a great deal of valuable information and allow you to start building a rapport. In this initial meeting, you are only gathering information. If you do not get to discuss yourself and your business during this initial meeting, you have still accomplished something.

E ssential

You have already networked with people without even realizing that is what you were doing. Networking is simply exchanging information, and takes place through many forms of communication: telephone, face-to-face conversations, e-mails, blogs, snail mail, etc. Consciously focusing your efforts on networking will make you more effective.

Asking good questions is an art form. Questions should be probing but not intrusive. Asking someone if they exercise will simply lead to a yes or no answer, while asking how they feel about an issue or event will lead to a discussion. Beginning your questions with "Why," "How," and "When" will help elicit more informative answers. Asking "Who" or "Where" questions might even lead you to names, places, or even contact numbers. Remember, networking is gathering information.

Setting Networking Objectives and Goals

Networking is like every other aspect of business: you need to determine exactly what you want to accomplish, both in the short and long term. If you are looking for more clients, how many do you need, and what criteria do they need to fit? Do you want males, females, young people, athletes, anyone with a flexible schedule? Answering these questions will give you focus and direction and will help you be able to clearly communicate your needs to others.

Before attending an event where you will interact with a large number of people, set goals for yourself so you do not get sidetracked or overwhelmed. You may set a goal to meet ten new people, engage them in conversation, and obtain three phone numbers or e-mail addresses. If you are new to networking, maybe you will try to speak to five people and obtain contact information from one of them.

Alert

When you do get to the point of asking for referrals, be specific about what you are looking for. People cannot help you if they are unsure of your needs. If you are looking for new personal-training clients, describe the type of person you want. Be clear about what you want and need, or you may not get it.

Getting the Most Out of Your Networking Efforts

Networking will allow you to develop a great deal of contacts and warm leads. It is your job to generate these leads into business. Use contact information to send out mailers or to gather more information. You can only do this if you keep a thorough, organized record of your leads, including the following information:

- Contact name
- Phone number or e-mail address
- Mailing address
- Occupation
- Hobbies or interests
- How and where you met
- Any other pertinent information

As soon as possible after meeting a contact, send them a note stating how much you enjoyed speaking with them and why. Make sure you include your contact information so they can get back in touch with you or pass your information on to someone else. This will keep you and your business fresh in their mind.

Networking Is Not Selling

Networking is about meeting people and building relationships. Your focus should be on gathering information that you can use or pass along to someone else who can use it. When you are networking, selling should be the furthest thing from your mind. When done properly, sales will happen as a natural course, but if it is your focus, you are missing the point of networking.

E ssential

When you engage people in conversation, their body language will tell more about what they think and feel than what they actually say. If they make eye contact and lean toward you, they are interested. If they look around, fidget, or lean away, they are not. If someone is uninterested or uncomfortable, politely end the conversation and move on.

Building Relationships

People prefer to do business with those they trust, so focus on developing relationships with everyone you meet. If they are not potential clients themselves, they probably know someone who could be. Ask questions and learn as much as you can about them and what they are about. Look for commonalities between you to increase the comfort level and give you more to talk about; anything to help people relate to and remember you for your personality, not just your career. Discuss hobbies and interests, and maybe even share a funny story. The more you have in common with someone, the better chance you have to continue the relationship. In turn, your new acquaintance could introduce you to someone else who has similar interests. You are now extending your network. The more you network, the larger your circle of influence will become. One person will introduce you to two people, who will each introduce you to two more, and so on.

Give Before You Receive

If you focus on helping others grow their businesses, it will eventually come back to you. For example, say you hire a newly licensed electrician to do work for you and are pleased with the job he did. You then give his name to several people you know who are looking for someone to do electrical work. That electrician may then turn around and refer the CEO of the next business he works for to you. If you help people, they will want to help you. That being said, your sole reason behind giving referrals should not be to get them in return. Selflessly helping others feels good and will always yield positive results.

Local Networking Groups

There are numerous associations or groups specializing in business development and networking. Their purpose is to give their members a formal opportunity to network with and learn from other professionals. When used properly, they can be an invaluable resource, especially if you feel unsure of yourself in this area.

 Fact

Over 40 percent of Americans ask their friends and family for advice when shopping for services. This makes word of mouth one of the most effective sources for business referrals. Are your clients talking about you? If so, what are they saying?

Networking groups are a great place to learn and hone your networking skills. You will receive newsletters, books, workshops, and other forms of training. The information you learn and the contacts you make can really help you grow your business. They are especially helpful if you are new in town or do not have a large warm market.

Organizations with Proven Track Records

For a fee of $200–$400, you can join a local networking group. These groups typically meet once a week and are an opportunity to meet people who can help you get referrals. One very popular group is the Business Network International (BNI). BNI was founded by networking guru Ivan Misner, and has been around for over twenty years. Their approach has been proven to be successful, and they currently have over 80 thousand members. For more information, log on to *www.bni.com*.

 Fact

The average person knows approximately 250 people. Every time you meet someone and build a relationship, you increase your list of potential clients by 250. Even if this person does not need or desire your services, there is a good chance one of the 250 people she knows will need you.

You can also join your local chapter of the Chamber of Commerce. The Chamber offers numerous opportunities for its members to meet and network with other professionals. In addition, your business will be listed on an online search engine where people interested in your services can look for businesses in their area. They also offer free seminars and extensive online information.

There may be other local groups in your area who charge a lesser fee, but they will likely be smaller and may not offer the extensive perks that the Chamber and BNI provide. Check the newspaper or yellow pages for local listings. If your time allows, you might consider joining a smaller group in addition to one of the more established groups. Just be careful not to overextend yourself.

Networking with Other Professionals

Interacting with other professionals or businesses is both rewarding and demanding. When another professional associates their name with your business, they are putting a great deal of trust in you. These relationships take time to cultivate but are worth the effort. They have a large pool of customers who will trust their advice if they refer them to you, but you must first prove yourself worthy of that trust.

Health Professionals

Developing a referral system with health professionals can dramatically boost your client base. Doctors, chiropractors, physical therapists, massage therapists, and mental health professionals see large numbers of people who could use your services. Their patients trust their judgment and will tend to go with what they suggest. In the same way, your clients trust your judgment and may ask you to recommend a health professional for various issues.

Establishing networking relationships with health professionals will require time and effort. It is difficult to walk into an office where you are not known, give your information, and have them agree to referrals. You will have to prove that you can do what you say you can. Sometimes you can accomplish this by finding health professionals who want to train with you. They will experience your skills and abilities firsthand, and may in turn be more likely to offer referrals. If this is not an option, ask your clients who have had success with you to speak to their health professionals. Try to set up a meeting or at least pass along some brochures and business cards. They may be more willing to meet with you knowing that you have helped one of their patients.

E ssential

Other fitness professionals can also be a great source of referrals. Look for people who specialize in a different area or population than you, or who are located in another part of the state. If you meet people who fall within their location and demographic, you can send them a referral, and they can do the same for you.

Other Business People

Even people who have nothing to do with your business can be great allies. If they believe in you and what you do, they can be a great source of referrals. Most likely they, too are looking for referrals and could benefit from a networking relationship.

Alert

When you are networking with other professionals, emphasize that you will be referring people to them as well. Show them how they will benefit from the relationship. Before you agree to this, be certain that you have confidence in the services they provide. You do not want to send your clients to someone who is incompetent or gives poor service.

You will benefit most from professionals who frequently interact with your target market. For example, if your target market is women in the thirty to fifty year age range, think about what types of professional services they use. Just about every woman gets her hair done, so why not network with a salon or spa owner near your business? You could leave your business cards and brochures in the salon and take hers to place in your facility. You could also come up with some type of joint promotion where her customers receive a discount from you, and your customers get a discount at the salon.

Trade Shows and Conferences

Trade shows and conferences are a great place to get your name in front of people in face-to-face meetings. They offer an opportunity to network in a cost-effective arena. You may choose to attend these events as a participant, or you could rent space as a vendor and set up a booth. Regardless of what event you attend and how you participate, make sure you arrive prepared to respond to any and all inquiries about your products and services.

Maximize Your Effectiveness

Make the best use of your time by attending events that are relevant to your business and will be attended by people who will be interested in what you do. This can mean many things. You may choose to participate in health fairs, business networking conferences, continuing education seminars; the list is endless. When you meet a promising prospect, request a business card. That way you will be able to contact them after the event and add them to your mailing list. Be conscientious about following up with them in a timely fashion. Lack of follow up or tardiness in following up can result in loss of business.

Remember that the people you speak to at these events will have also been approached by countless others trying to sell their services. Find a way to distinguish yourself from the crowd and re-establish contact as soon as possible so you stay at the forefront of their minds.

Be Prepared

If you are going to spend your valuable time at these events, you will want to make the most of it. Before you go, practice what you plan to say. You will be speaking to many people, but for short periods of time, so keep it concise. Bring your press kit and any samples of your products you have. Anything you can give people to take with them will help keep your name in their minds. Do remember, however, that you are networking and networking is not sales. Try to focus equally on how you can help others and encourage reciprocal relationships.

Public Relations

Public relations are a way to establish relationships and develop your warm market within your community. There are plenty of public relation opportunities, you simply have to look for them and be prepared to participate. During these events, make information available to spectators and participants and have a means for interested parties to leave their contact information so you can place them on your mailing list.

Community Events

Think about how you can align yourself with events in your community. You may sponsor a town athletic team or a local event. It is a way to be involved in the community, and will also get your name out there. You do not have to be the lead sponsor if the financial obligations are too great; just being a part of the event is enough. Worthwhile events include road races, walk-a-thons, blood drives, or even food collections. Anything that puts you and your business in front of people is constructive.

If you don't have the money to sponsor an event, volunteer your time. This is oftentimes more needed and appreciated than financial support. Plus, volunteering fosters relationships. Consider wearing clothes with your company name and handing out information or placing it in a well-traveled area.

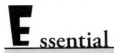

If the town is having a walk-a-thon, you can volunteer to put the participants through a warm-up routine before the event. You will be giving people a sample of your knowledge and services as well as putting a face to your business name.

Do What You Enjoy

If you have hobbies or interests outside of training, capitalize on them. Start or join a group where you will meet and connect with others who share your interests. Join a softball team or a dance class. Take an art or cooking class. Start a book club. Learn something new.

Networking is easier and more enjoyable when you are doing it in a relaxed environment with people you can relate to.

Common Mistakes

Just as there are many good ways to network, there are also ways you can make costly mistakes. You may not pay in a literal way, but you can lose business and damage your reputation.

Selling When You Should Be Nurturing

Coming on too strong is a sure way to scare people away. If you are pushing to sell instead of listening and learning, you will accomplish very little. Remember, people do business with those they like and trust. If people feel positively toward you, they will want to work with you. They will not feel positively if they think you have an agenda and are only out to further your own career and goals.

Not Delivering What You Promised

Networking is based on trust and relationships. If you break that trust, you will lose the relationship and any referrals you may have received. The quickest way to do this is failing to follow through on a promise or agreement. Whether this is an oversight or an intentional act, if you do not keep your word, people will not want to be involved with you. If you say you will do something, do it and do it promptly. Otherwise you will be viewed as unreliable. Even if what you promised is something small like a phone call, failure to follow through will result in negative feelings and may cause you to lose the relationship. The bottom line is that you need to go above and beyond for the people in your network.

Chapter 13

Professionalism

Upholding a high standard of professionalism is of the utmost importance to your reputation as a personal trainer. The industry has grown tremendously over the past twenty years, and in order to continue this growth, trainers need to portray themselves as the professionals they have become. Some trainers mistakenly think that because they are working in a gym environment where people are relaxed and in sweats, the standards for professional behavior are somehow relaxed as well. This could not be further from the truth. Personal trainers have a responsibility to act with honesty, integrity, courtesy, and ethics, both in and outside of the workplace.

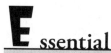

Professional conduct begins with a firm handshake, eye contact, and a smile. In the first few moments of meeting someone, you can start building a rapport. Learn names and use them. This shows people that you care about and are interested in them.

Look, Speak, and Act as a Professional

Peoples' perceptions of you will have a significant impact on your level of success as a personal trainer. Human beings are very visual and really do judge books by their covers. In today's increasingly superficial society, appearances are increasingly important. When consumers make purchases, they consider the way the product looks just as important as how it functions. In the same way, potential clients will make judgments about you based on how you present yourself.

Dress for Success

Because of the physical nature of the personal training business, it is not practical to wear a suit to work. However, you are working, so the clothes you wear should fit certain criteria. Khaki shorts or pants look nice, though athletic shorts or pants are acceptable if you tend to be very physical during your workouts. Collared golf shirts look uniform and professional, but long- or short-sleeved T-shirts are also okay. Placing your company logo on your shirts is a nice touch and adds to the professional look. Be careful with tank tops and cutoffs, as they can look shabby. Sneakers are appropriate for footwear, but should be kept clean and replaced frequently. The bottom line is, you should be well-kept, with neat hair, a clean shave, and clothes that are clean and in order. If you look professional, people will be more likely to think of and treat you as a professional.

 **Alert**

Clothing and footwear must never appear worn or tattered. A properly attired trainer looks clean and neat, not like a college student rolling out of bed late for class. Many of the people you train will be professionals, and they will not want to hire a trainer who looks like an amateur.

If you are working for a health club, they may provide you with a uniform. Some larger clubs will even provide their trainers with sneakers or offer a clothing stipend. If there is no uniform, the company handbook will likely dictate a dress code. When in doubt, observe what the other employees are wearing, then take it to the next level so you stand out. You want people to notice how professional you look. Taking extra care with your appearance will give the impression that you are willing to go the extra mile with your clients, and that you are not afraid to put forth a good effort.

Professional Demeanor

Whether you are meeting a new member for the first time, speaking to current members on the fitness floor, or training a client, your demeanor speaks volumes about who you are. People, potential clients especially, are watching your body language, facial expressions, and actions. In some ways, it's like being on stage or auditioning for a part.

E ssential

Professionalism is the first step to obtaining a new client. A potential client can decide whether or not they will purchase your services by their first interaction with you. If you do not look, speak, and act in a way that portrays you in a good light, you will not attract much business.

Verbal Communication

Proper verbal communication literally speaks volumes about who you are. Present yourself as a well-spoken professional, and people will treat you as one. This encompasses a great deal. The most basic guidelines are to speak slowly, clearly, and use proper grammar, not slang.

Remember that you are speaking to clients, not your friends. While your clients may be casual with you, you must retain a level of professionalism at all times. Use clean language and proper terminology. During your sessions, refrain from discussing clients with other clients. Doing so will give your clients the impression that you do not respect client-trainer confidentiality, and will result in a loss of trust.

Even if your clients curse or use inappropriate language, refrain from following suit. During your training sessions, potential clients are often within earshot. You may think you are having a private conversation, but you never know who is listening. If potential clients overhear you speaking in an inappropriate or unprofessional way, they may decide not to hire you.

Portraying a Professional Attitude

While people will make their initial assessments of you based on how you look, their lasting impressions will be formed by your attitude. Professionalism is about character. If you exhibit a positive outlook, and truly put your clients first, they will take notice and respect you. If, on the other hand, you do not take your clients seriously or are just in it for the money, that will also become evident, and they will not want to work with you.

Take Pride in Your Work

If you truly take pride in your work, you will strive to give your clients 100 percent every day. You will push to be the best, provide top-notch customer service, and go the extra mile for your clients and yourself. Take every opportunity to go above and beyond, and the positive feelings will flow.

Continuously adding to your knowledge base is one way to demonstrate your work ethic. It shows that you will put forth effort and do what it takes to serve your clients. Increase your knowledge and stay current by reading journals and books related to the field. Attend seminars and workshops or take an online course.

Taking pride in your work also means being open to constructive criticism and correction. If you really want to be the best, you must be willing to change and grow. Seek out feedback from your clients, and if you work for someone, your employer. Use the responses as a way to improve yourself and your programs.

Commit Yourself to Your Clients and Their Goals

While you do need to be concerned with running a successful business, your primary concern should be serving the best interests of your clients. Happy, satisfied clients will create a successful business for you. Focus on each clients' individual needs. Make his goal your own, and give 100 percent to helping him reach those goals.

When you are truly invested in helping your clients achieve success, they will know and appreciate it. And more importantly, they will tell others.

The Client-Trainer Relationship

The relationship between trainer and client can be quite intense. You are working closely with people for what can end up being many years. During this time, they will experience numerous ups and downs in their lives, many of which they will share with you: marriage, pregnancy, job changes, loss of loved ones, and so on. The nature of the trainer-client relationship is physical, mental, and emotional. You are being placed in a position of trust, and must take great care to respect that position.

Fact

The National Council on Strength and Fitness produces an extensive code of ethics for the client-trainer relationship, including professional ethics, societal responsibilities, conflicts of interests, and trainer conduct and practices. See the entire NCSF code of conduct at ✑www.ncsf.org/boardcert/ethics.aspx.

Building Rapport

Rapport can be defined as a relationship of mutual trust and understanding between two people. The nature of personal training requires trainers to establish rapport with their clients in order to be successful. Gaining the confidence of your clients is of the utmost importance. If they do not trust you, they will not confide in you, and you will not be able to help them completely. You must prove yourself to be honest, trustworthy, and reliable before people will share with you their hopes, fears, successes, and shortcomings. Establishing these types of relationships takes time, patience, and consideration.

Another aspect of building rapport is working to understand where your client is coming from. If you can see life through your clients' eyes, you will have a better idea how to guide them toward success. Be mentally present during every session. Really listen when clients share things with you, and read between the lines when necessary.

Know How to Listen

Listening to your clients will help you understand what makes them tick. When you understand what drives them, you can help them achieve success. Unless the issues are directly related to personal training, be cautious about offering advice. Keep your opinions to yourself unless you are asked. Most people can work out their own problems by talking about them, and if your clients wish to hear your opinion, they will say so.

Personal Training Gets Personal

The longer you work with your clients, the more intimately you will get to know them. As you build trust and rapport, they will begin to divulge information about their personal lives. You will be amazed at the things your clients choose to share with you.

In order to help people achieve their physical goals you will likely have to address some mental and emotional issues.

Recognizing and Respecting Boundaries

As a personal trainer, you are in a trusted position. You are a coach and mentor, and your clients will look up to you. Avoid taking advantage of your position. It is only natural that at some point, physical attraction may occur between trainer and client. It may or may not be mutual, but it should be taken seriously. Becoming romantically involved with a client is bad for business. You will not only lose that client, you will mar your reputation. This is even more of an issue if one or both parties are married or in committed relationships. This sends a negative message about your character and ethics, and is simply a disaster waiting to happen. If you are employed by a health club, they will likely have a strict policy pertaining to these situations. Trainers are often prohibited from becoming romantically involved with members, as it can lead to loss of business if the relationship ends badly.

Alert

It is not unusual for clients to develop crushes on their trainers. Most personal trainers take good care of themselves and are physically fit. They are also charismatic and personable. People are drawn to them because of it, and these qualities contribute to their success. However, to allow a crush to be acted upon is unwise and unprofessional.

Respecting Your Clients' Personal Space

Personal training is a hands-on profession, and involves close physical contact with clients. Some clients will be more comfortable with this than others, and it is important to work within each clients' individual comfort zone. Failure to do so could result in loss of the client, or worse, a sexual harassment suit. Remember, communication is key.

Sometimes you will need to show a client where a muscle is or take them through a movement. Ask permission before touching them, and explain what you are going to do ahead of time. Some people will not give physical contact a second thought, while others will be bothered by it. Until you know your client well, do not assume that it is okay to put your hands on them unless you ask first.

Reading Your Client's Cues and Body Language

While it is important to listen to what your clients say, pay even closer attention to their body language and non-verbal cues. Look at their postures, gestures, facial expressions, and other physical signs to see what messages they are sending. If your client feels uncomfortable or nervous, they may be too shy or embarrassed to tell you. You need to pick up on it yourself. They may fidget, lean or look away, speak more quickly, turn red, start to sweat, or display some other behavior. If you find yourself in this situation, stop and evaluate what you are doing. Try to correct the problem without causing the client further embarrassment. If you are unsuccessful, you may need to ask them directly how you can make them more comfortable. The longer you work with your clients, the better you will understand them and the easier it will be to interact.

Maintaining Confidentiality

Clients share a tremendous amount of personal information with their trainers, making confidentiality a huge issue. In addition to their medical history, clients talk to their trainers about their goals, fears, stressors, family life, work, and a great deal of other personal issues. This is an honor, but may also be a burden. It is your professional responsibility to keep the information you are given between you and your client.

Sign an Agreement

Protecting your clients' privacy should be at the top of your list among safety and success. Developing and implementing a confidentiality agreement for your clients will show that you respect and honor their privacy. Putting it on paper reinforces the fact that you are a professional who is worthy of their trust, and contributes to an open, honest relationship.

Your clients are sharing with you their medical history, their hopes, fears, successes, and failures. For some, this will be easier than others. If you create a sense of comfort with your clients, over time even the most hesitant will come to trust you. Having a signed, written agreement can speed up this process by putting clients at ease. They will feel more comfortable opening up and revealing private information if they are guaranteed it will stay with you. Working to achieve their goals is difficult enough without having to worry about what they should or should not discuss with you.

Professionalism Outside of the Workplace

The longer you are in this profession, the more people will come to know you. People will begin to recognize you outside of your place of business, even when you do not see or recognize them. To avoid embarrassment or loss of potential business, you need to maintain a certain level of professionalism in any public situation.

Interacting With Clients After Hours

In any job, people find their professional relationships becoming more personal and gravitating toward friendships. It is part of being human. While the lines between business and friendship may become fuzzy, there still need to be lines. First and foremost, you have a business to maintain. Your behavior, even after hours, should be beyond reproach.

Having good working relationships with clients is a positive for creating a successful business. You may decide to take a good client out to celebrate a birthday or other special occasion. This is a nice way to go the extra mile with your clients, and will likely be greatly appreciated. Be sure to enjoy yourself while remembering that you are entertaining for business purposes. If you behave as casually as you would with your friends, you may embarrass yourself.

Always Be Prepared

You never know when you will meet your next client. When meeting someone new, always remember that he could be your next client. Being a professional at all times will help in your efforts to obtain new clients. If you remain in work mode even when you are not at work, you will present yourself as more professional. Once again, this includes attire, verbal communication, and overall behavior. That first impression will speak volumes about you. Even if the people you meet are not interested in your services for themselves, they may pass your name along to someone who is interested.

Carry business cards so you can hand them out to people who show interest in your services. If someone asks you for a card, supply them with a few extra so they can hand them out to people they know. If you have brochures that you can keep handy, you can pass those along as well. Most importantly, have a pen and paper or PDA with you at all times so you can take down the contact information of potential customers. This way you can be proactive and contact them first, in addition to adding them to your mailing or contact list.

Chapter 14

Initial Appointments

The first time you meet with your clients is one of the most significant appointments you will spend with them. The majority of this time will be spent talking and gathering information. The safety of the client and effectiveness of the programs you develop will be contingent upon what you learn during this time. You have between thirty and ninety minutes to gain their trust, get to know them and their goals, and show them how working with you will help them achieve their goals.

The Health Screening

The first task during the initial appointment is taking a thorough medical history. Request that your clients arrive with the forms already completed, or arrive fifteen minutes prior to their scheduled time so you don't have to spend valuable time filling out paperwork. If you can have the information returned to you before the appointment, you will have more time to review it and prepare.

Why Perform a Health Screening?

Health screenings are important for several reasons. First, they assist you in determining if a client is healthy enough to begin an exercise program. While you may not expect it, there will be times when people who are unfit to exercise will try to hire you to train them. They may be in denial or simply unaware of the severity of their problem. Regardless, you are responsible for knowing enough to refuse to train them. Health screenings are also a means by which to uncover any conditions that might require a modified program or special considerations, such as low back pain, asthma, or even depression. Take an extreme example of an apparently healthy middle-aged man who wishes to begin training with you. Unbeknownst to you, this man has had two heart attacks and is on blood pressure and cholesterol medication. He has also had shoulder surgery and a knee replacement. If you were to begin training him without performing a health screening, you could easily have him performing exercises that could cause him harm. If, on the other hand, you sit down with him beforehand and obtain a complete medical history, you will be armed with this information and be able to take the proper steps toward implementing a safe and effective program (once he has been cleared by his doctor).

Not everyone will need a doctor's clearance, but if your client has experienced any of the following situations, she might want to make an appointment with a doctor before getting started with you:

- A family history of diabetes, heart disease, or other cardiovascular disease under the age of fifty-five
- Diagnosed with heart problems or has had heart surgery
- Diabetes
- Taking medication for high blood pressure, heart disease, or diabetes
- Other medical conditions such as arthritis, osteoporosis, heart murmur, allergies, or asthma
- Pain or swelling in the joints
- Pregnant or lactating
- Problems with dizziness or fainting spells
- Recovering from any type of injury or illness

The Health Screening Form

If you are employed by a health club or other fitness facility, they will likely have their own forms and protocols for health screenings. If you are self-employed, you will need to develop your own. At a minimum, your forms should request the following information:

- Age
- Gender
- Occupation
- Exercise history
- Health issues
- Medications
- Allergies
- Past injuries or surgeries
- Current injuries
- Family medical history
- Other habits such as caffeine, alcohol, or recreational drugs

The more complete and inclusive the form, the better equipped you will be to design an individualized program. This information will help you assess risk factors and special needs. Appendix A contains a sample health questionnaire.

The Physical Activity Readiness Questionnaire (PAR Q) was developed by the British Columbia Ministry of Health and modified by the Canadian Society for Exercise Physiology (CSEP) to identify people for whom exercise is very risky or not appropriate, and those who should be cleared by a physician prior to beginning a program. They have given permission for people to copy the document with the stipulation that you use the entire form. You may download a copy from the CSEP at *www.csep.ca*. Click on "publications" then on "fitness publications." The PAR Q does not take the place of a full health history form, but can be a nice complement.

Essential

Request that your clients keep you updated on any changes in their health status or medications, then document this information in their records. Once or twice a year, formally review the health screening form with your clients to ensure it is current and accurate. If they report major changes, ask them to complete another form. Much can happen in a year.

Referral to a Physician

There may be instances where the health screening reveals a condition that warrants referral to a physician, such as an uncontrolled medical condition or an unhealed injury. If this does occur, it is unethical and irresponsible to continue training the client unless he's first cleared by a medical doctor. To cover yourself legally, request a letter from his doctor clearing him for exercise and specifying what, if anything, they say he should not be doing. Some trainers have a form used specifically for this purpose, to ensure they obtain all necessary information. See Appendix A.

E ssential

> You will notice a big difference between the mindset and capabilities of clients who are new to exercising, and those who are returning from a break. Beginning exercisers are probably just hoping to make it through your session, while those getting back from a break will want to pick up where they left off.

There will be times when a client has needs that your background and experiences do not equip you to handle. A client may be recovering from back surgery or have a serious eating disorder. When these situations present themselves, it is your responsibility to refer the client to someone who can work with her issues. If you are feeling uncomfortable in any way, do not ignore your instincts. It is better to lose a client than hurt her and find yourself being sued.

Conducting a Thorough Interview

The more information you gather during the initial appointment, the better equipped you will be to serve your client. Keep in mind, however, that if you have just met the client, he may feel apprehensive about providing you with personal information. Explaining the purpose of the interview ahead of time may help put your clients at ease and make them more willing to open up.

Your Clients' Lifestyle

In addition to a health history questionnaire, many trainers will also ask their clients to complete a lifestyle questionnaire. The information gathered here is used to determine the current and past levels of physical activity, eating habits, and other lifestyle factors that may influence compliance and success. Armed with this data, you will be better equipped to address individual needs and create a personalized program. Once again, if the form is completed before the appointment, it will save valuable time. If upon reviewing the document you find you have more specific questions, you can ask them during the appointment.

There are six main components of a lifestyle questionnaire:

- Exercise history and current activity level
- Occupation
- Hobbies
- Nutritional habits
- Mental health
- Support systems

Learning about your clients' past and present exercise habits will give you a great deal of insight into where to begin and how to progress. Ask for details about the types of exercise performed in the past and the intensity at which they were performed. Did they run, swim, dance, weight lift? Were they a competitive athlete, and if so, at what level did they compete? People who were competitive athletes will tend to want a more intense workout than those who were not. What do they do now for exercise? What forms of exercise do they most enjoy? Everyone's attitudes toward exercise will be different as well. For some it will be a chore, while others will look forward to it as a stress reliever or down time. It is helpful to know where each client is coming from. Try to obtain as much detailed information as possible without sounding like you are interrogating the client.

What your client does for work will also play a role in their program. The client who sits behind a desk all day will have different physical and dietary needs than the client who owns and operates a moving company. You also want to find out what kind of hours he is working so you can best determine when he can exercise and when he needs to rest.

Asking your clients about their hobbies may seem silly or not relevant, but this could not be further from the truth. Your clients' hobbies will give you further insight into their personalities and overall level of physical activity. A client who enjoys outdoor activities may want to exercise outside as much as possible. You will want to incorporate this into her program so she finds enjoyment in her exercise routine. Learning about what your clients do in their spare time might also help you find common interests that you share and give you things to talk about.

Remember to inquire about nutritional habits on your lifestyle forms. Have they dieted in the past? What types of diets have they tried? Are they dieting now? What do they typically eat in a day? A full program takes into account all aspects of health. Your clients' success will be limited if they have poor eating habits.

Stress level and support systems also play key roles in the success or failure of a program. People who can deal well with stress and have adequate support from family and friends will be able to persevere, and will be more compliant than those with excessive amounts of stress and no support system.

Alert

Consider all aspects of your clients' lives, not just the time they spend in the gym. What they eat and how much they move during the day will have an enormous impact on their health, appearance, and well-being. A client who spends two hours a day in the gym, then eats and drinks all night will sabotage her health and her program.

Your Clients' Expectations and Goals

When your clients contact you to set up an initial appointment, they will give you a vague idea why they want to meet with you. They will typically say something like, "I want to lose weight" or "I want to get back into shape." You may get a bit more information, but usually not much more. The interview is the time to get specific about precisely what they wish to accomplish. How much weight do they want to lose, and in what time frame? What does being in shape mean to them? Once you understand where the client is coming from and what they are hoping for, you can set the long- and short-term goals.

At this point, most clients will have a high level of enthusiasm and excitement. They are ready to make changes in their lives and are feeling pretty motivated. In some cases, they are so enthusiastic that they will have unrealistic expectations of you and of themselves. You may have a client who expects to lose twenty pounds in a month, or bench press the weight he lifted in college, on the first day. These are unrealistic and unsafe expectations, and you must find a way to convey that message without wrecking the client's enthusiasm. Take this time to educate your clients about how the body works, as well as what they can expect from their programs. Use the gist of their expectations to help them set realistic, achievable goals with a reasonable time frame.

Reviewing and Signing the Legal Contracts

Before beginning any program, you must cover yourself legally. There are risks involved with exercise, even with the healthiest individuals. It is your responsibility to make your clients aware of these risks, and require that they sign both informed consent and liability waivers. This can be an uncomfortable moment for you as a trainer. Just be sure to explain yourself thoroughly and answer any questions before asking your clients to sign the paperwork. You will diligently work to provide a safe and effective program, but accidents do happen.

Informed Consent Form

The purpose of informed consent is to confirm that the client understands what they will be doing, and the benefits and risks involved in participating in an exercise program. No matter how healthy a person may be, there are always risks associated with exercise. This form will also explain the client's responsibility to report any unusual symptoms they may experience during their sessions such as dizziness, chest pain, or unusual pain in joints or muscles.

When they have read the document, ask if they have any questions or concerns about what they have read. Emphasize that you are willing to clarify anything they may feel unclear or unsure of. When you feel certain your client has a complete understanding of the form, request their signature and give them a copy to take home.

Liability Waiver

Some trainers will use the informed consent form as a liability waiver as well. This is a mistake. While the two may appear to be the same, there are differences, and you should require your clients to sign both to ensure you are fully covered. The informed consent simply states that the client is healthy and fit to exercise, understands the risks involved in what he is doing, and is willing to participate. By signing the liability waiver, the client releases you and your business of responsibility for any injuries or damages that may incur while participating in a session or exercising at your facility. They know and accept the risks, and are assuming responsibility for their actions.

Pretesting

You may or may not have time during the first appointment to perform your baseline testing. It will depend on how long the interview portion takes, your proficiency at testing, and how much time you allow for initial consultations. If you really want to get the testing done at your first meeting, you may consider allotting ninety minutes for your initial consultations. This allows you to have a program planned and ready to implement for your second appointment.

Why Testing Is Important

There are several reasons to perform exercise testing. The first is to assess risk. If you take a client's blood pressure and it is through the roof, you will obviously not be continuing with the session. Instead, you will refer that person to their physician. If you had not performed this assessment, and instead had gone right into a workout, your client's blood pressure could have continued to rise and they may have had a stroke during their session.

Testing will also provide you with information that will help you develop a program to meet your clients' needs in a more individualized way. You will be able to see where each clients' strengths and weaknesses lie and what you need to work on. The client who can run a mile in six minutes, but cannot perform a pushup, needs to spend more time working on upper-body strength.

At some point, your client's motivation may start to lessen. You can use both pretesting and posttesting as a motivational tool to show them where they are improving or where they need to put in more effort. Re-evaluating your clients every four to six weeks will also allow you to assess the effectiveness of your program design. If your client is not showing improvement, you may need to make some modifications.

E ssential

Charting progress is much more precise when you have numbers to base it on. Six months down the line, if you have not tested, you can tell your client she is stronger and has more stamina. If you do test, you can tell her she improved her upper body strength by thirty percent.

Some clients will not want to be tested because they are embarrassed, anxious, or uncomfortable. When you find yourself in this situation, try reiterating the benefits of testing. If they are still unwilling, respect their wishes and do not pressure them to comply. They may eventually come around, and if they do not, then find other ways to chart progress. You may simply show them their chart and compare their exercise program on day one with their program six months later.

Types of Tests

There are countless indicators of health and fitness and numerous tests you can perform to measure them. Some tests are quick and easy, while others take more time and effort. You may choose to assess all of these factors or only a few, depending on your client and the equipment you have access to. Whatever evaluations you choose to perform should be carried out in the following order, or the results may be inaccurate:

- Anthropometric tests: height, weight, and the circumference of certain body parts
- Body weight
- Body composition
- Blood pressure
- Resting heart rate
- Cardiovascular endurance: 30-second or 1-minute step test
- Muscular strength: 1 RM bench press
- Muscular endurance: push up test
- Flexibility: sit and reach test

The tools you will use and the tests you perform will depend on your clients' needs and the equipment at your disposal. Trainers in health clubs will have more equipment at their disposal than trainers who work in-home. For example, there are several different ways to perform body-composition tests. The method that provides the most accurate results is hydrostatic weighing. The problems with the test are that it requires special equipment and is expensive and time-consuming to perform. Skin-fold calipers are less precise than hydrostatic weighing, but are also the least-expensive tools with which to perform body-composition analysis. They are small enough to carry with you, and with a little practice, you can become proficient at testing your clients' body fat. They serve the purpose of allowing you to establish a baseline measurement and chart progress, even if the results are not completely accurate. Bioelectrical impedance analysis (BIA) is another form of body-composition testing. It works by sending an imperceptible electrical impulse through the body. The speed of the impulse passing through the body will vary depending on the client's lean body mass. This method is less expensive than hydrostatic weighing, but more expensive than skin-fold calipers, and is the least-accurate form of testing. If you do not have any of these tools, you can use anthropometric tests that only require the use of a tape measure. You do not need expensive tools to perform your evaluation. Just be sure that you use the same methods of evaluation for both pretesting and posttesting so you can accurately assess progress.

The American College of Sports Medicine has published a book titled *ACSM's Guidelines for Exercise Testing and Prescription*. This book contains detailed, up-to-date information on all aspects of exercise testing, including how to perform tests, how to interpret the results, and much more. It is small enough to carry with you as a reference and is a great tool for every personal trainer.

Discussing the Results with Your Client

Talking with your clients about the results of their testing can be a challenge. It requires you to display empathy and sensitivity. Many times people are more out of shape than they realized, and this is a big reality check. Your clients may feel discouraged or overwhelmed by their results. Explain how the program you will design will help them get where they want to go, and that you will be with them every step of the way. It may also be helpful to emphasize how many of your other clients have been in this same situation, but were successful due to hard work and dedication. Do everything you can to ensure that your client leaves feeling optimistic and ready to take on the challenge.

Financial Matters

Talking about money can be difficult and uncomfortable, but it is necessary. To avoid confusion, address the issue clearly and candidly. It is helpful to have your fees and policies in writing and send them to your client before your first meeting. You can then answer any questions they have, and request that they sign off that they agree to and understand the fees and policies.

Consultation Fees

Your fees for the initial consultation may be different than what you charge for a regular appointment. Some trainers do not charge for the initial consultation, and use it more as an interview for both the client and the trainer. Others will charge an added fee for the initial appointment, due to the increased time, paperwork, and planning required of the trainer.

If you decide to charge a consultation fee, explain to your client when they make the appointment that most of the time will be spent talking, and little, if any, will be spent exercising. Be sure to inform them that you'll be performing an evaluation to assess their level of fitness. If you fail to do this, your client may assume that they will jump right into exercising, and they will be disappointed when the time comes. Present the consultation as an added service. Explain that they are not required to participate in the interview or testing portions, but that it is a valuable tool and will assist you in better serving them. If your client chooses not to participate, you will still need to have all forms signed and completed before beginning their session.

Alert

Offering free consultations is not the best business practice. Training is about helping people, but it is also about making a living, so you may want to think twice about giving away your valuable time. You can also diminish the perceived value of your services if there is no fee attached.

Discussing Your Payment and Cancellation Policies

You may have included a form in your informational packet that listed your fees and cancellation policies. If you did not, take this time to provide your client with a copy. Explain when and how you expect to be paid. Some trainers accept checks and credit cards, while others do not. Some wish to be paid at the time the appointment is made, and others will accept payment after the appointment. You also need to inform your client of how much notice you require for a cancelled appointment. Be as clear and specific as possible and answer questions as they arise. When you feel your client understands your expectations, request their signature. Provide them with a copy and put the form in their file.

Selling Future Appointments

Your client may arrive at your initial appointment with the idea that she'll be given a program, then do it on her own. Or she may not come with any idea of how often she'll work with you. This is the perfect time to show your client how much she needs you, because she has just finished her fitness evaluation. If you want her to see you on a regular basis, you must sell her on the value of your services. Explain why your expertise makes you capable of helping her accomplish her goals more quickly than she could on her own. It is not necessary to pressure her. Simply educate her about the value of your services and what you have to offer. Then go over your packages and the options available to her.

Preparing for the Next Appointment

Once you have scheduled the next appointment, give your client an idea of what they will be doing and what training with you will be like. Many people will feel nervous or unsure, and will appreciate your effort to put their mind at ease. Assure them that while they will exert themselves, the workouts will be tailored to their skill and ability level. Just because they saw your last client groaning in pain, does not mean they will be doing the same. Fitness is a process, and this is the first step.

Your Clients' Homework

Training with you is not even half the battle for your clients. They must be consistently diligent and disciplined in order to achieve their goals. Send the message to your clients that their habits and behaviors when they are not with you will contribute more to their success than the hour or two a week they spend at your facility. If you expect them to keep a food or exercise log, now is the time to discuss it. Explain the importance of accountability and how this can affect their exercise outcome. They may be more willing to comply if they understand the reasoning behind your request. If keeping a log is too much for a client or they are simply unwilling to do it, give them something concrete to accomplish before the next time they see you.

Even if it is as simple as walking for ten minutes for three days, you will be sending the message that they need to do work on their own.

Your Own Homework

You have obtained a great deal of information during this initial appointment, and have a lot to consider when writing your program. While the results should all be in writing, do not rely solely on this. Write down the program as soon as possible after your appointment, so the details are fresh in your mind. If you wait until the day before you meet with the client again, you could have forgotten the feelings and instincts you felt during the consultation. This is some of your most valuable information and should not be neglected or ignored.

Chapter 15

Components of a Program

There are six main components to an exercise program: warm-up, core training, resistance training, cardiovascular training, cooldown, and stretching. Every well-balanced program contains these components, but in different degrees. The marathon runner will spend more time performing cardiovascular training than the high school football player. The client recovering from back surgery will spend more time performing core training than the modern dancer. Your challenge is to create the best program possible for each client, taking into account factors such as health, lifestyle, and goals. You can accomplish this task by understanding the theory and application of each training component.

Warm-Up

The warm-up should last between five and ten minutes, and is a great time to gather information from your client and get up to speed on what has happened since the last time you met. Because you may not see someone for a week or more, a great deal can transpire between appointments. You need to assess how physically and mentally prepared they are for the impending exercise. This is the time to ascertain how they are feeling and what they have done since they last saw you. By doing so, you can make any necessary modifications to the workout you planned. You can also use this time to explain what they can expect during the upcoming workout; what you will be focusing on and some of the exercises they will perform.

Why Your Client Should Warm-Up

The warm-up helps your clients prepare for their sessions physically and mentally. It decreases the risk of injury by increasing temperature and blood flow to the muscles. During this time, the body will take oxygen from the abdomen and send it to the muscles to increase oxygen supply. You are also giving your client time to gain mental focus and prepare for the rigors of the workout. If you neglect the warm-up, you are asking your client to go from zero to sixty in under a minute, which is both unsafe and uncomfortable.

Warming-Up at Home and in the Gym

The difference between getting your client warmed-up at home and in the gym is the equipment you may use. In the gym, you will have cardiovascular equipment at your disposal, while some clients who train in-home may not have these types of machines. This is not a problem. All you really need for a great warm-up is a stability ball, medicine ball, resistance bands, and your imagination. Your objective for the warm-up is to prepare the body for the upcoming exercise. It does not have to be too demanding, it just needs to mimic the types of exercises the client will be performing. You can increase your client's heart rate by having her step up and down on a bottom stair while she is holding dumbbells. If she will be performing a bench press, pushups are a good warm-up to prepare the chest muscles for the increased resistance.

Core and Balance Training

Core and balance training will help your clients both in their workouts and in their everyday lives. Incorporating these components into your programs will help your clients gain balance, stability, and strength. You can integrate core and balance training into any of the other parts of the workout. This is where you really get to use your imagination and fun equipment like bands, balls, foam rollers, Bosu balls, and dumbbells. If you are unfamiliar with the ins and outs of core and balance training, consider taking a course to increase your proficiency. Perform Better offers seminars and instructional DVDs on these topics for a reasonable price. Trainers who neglect these components of the workout are not providing their clients with a complete program. In addition to the benefits your clients will gain from this type of training, they will reduce their risk of injury if you utilize them properly.

What Is Core Training?

The core consists of the abdominal and deep back musculature. Core training is important because all movement originates in the core. If the core muscles are weak, your clients' movements will be inefficient. Over time this can result in chronic back pain and other injuries. This will also inhibit the client's ability to progress in other areas.

Developing a program that involves the core muscles will help your client progress to more advanced exercises. Many people think that by working their abs they are performing core training. This is not really what core training is about. Core training is much more complex and has more to do with the fact that the deep back muscles stabilize the spine during each and every movement. If these muscles fail to do their job, you will not be able to maximize your strength. Some examples of core training include stability ball bench press and stability ball crunch.

 Alert

Do not utilize core training unless you have received instruction in this area. If you don't know what you are doing, you could cause more harm than if you leave this component out of the program. You will also be acting outside your scope of practice and opening yourself up to a lawsuit. It is safer to wait until you have attended a workshop.

Improving Balance

Balance is important in everyday life because people walk upright. The simple act of walking involves balance. Just look at a toddler who is walking for the first time or an elderly person who fears falling when he walks. We take balance for granted, but it's not just athletes who need to work on it. At any point, your client could accidentally step off the curb or trip over her child's toys. With good balance she may avoid a fall, potential injury, and embarrassment.

Balance training can be as simple as asking your client to stand on an Airex pad while she performs her shoulder exercises. There are many tools you can purchase to assist with balance training, but the simple act of moving from two feet to one foot involves balance. Toys will keep your client interested and engaged but they are not a requirement.

Resistance Training

Resistance training may also be referred to as weight or strength training. These terms can be used interchangeably when discussing resistance training. They all refer to the practice of using increasingly heavier weights to overload the muscles, causing them to get stronger. The resistance component of the workout is the one that comes to mind when most people think of personal training.

E ssential

Most potential clients who approach you will express their desire to weight train. Men might want to bulk up or get stronger. A woman might say she wants to tone but not get big or firm up her thighs and butt. These types of goals can be reached with a properly designed resistance program.

Different Methods of Resistance Training

Resistance training may be performed using a variety of tools. There are machines, free weights, dumbbells, resistance bands, body weight, medicine balls, or even cans of soup. Anything that can load the muscle to the point of fatigue will do the trick. You can separate the types of resistance training equipment into three basic categories: isometric, isotonic, and isokinetic.

Isometric training, also referred to as static training, involves contracting the muscles without moving the joints. For example, you would instruct your client to contract the quadriceps (thigh) muscles by squeezing and holding for ten seconds. This form of training is typically used in a rehabilitation setting. Your healthy clients will find this form of training too easy and will become bored fairly quickly.

 Fact

You may choose to train muscular strength, muscular endurance, or both. Muscular strength is the maximum amount of force a muscle can produce against resistance for one repetition, while muscular endurance is the muscle's ability to continuously exert force against resistance. Your clients' goals will determine how much of the program is dedicated to increasing muscular strength versus muscular endurance.

Isotonic, or dynamic, training is the most popular form of training. Dynamic training is what typically comes to mind when someone mentions strength training. You perform this type of training when you use dumbbells, free weights, machines, or other equipment to exert a force on the muscle while the joint is moving through a motion. Dynamic training can increase both muscular strength and endurance, and can be an exciting way to train clients.

Isokinetic means "same speed." This form of training is similar to isotonic training in that it involves shortening and lengthening contractions. The difference is that equipment is used to keep the speed of movement the same throughout the movement, regardless of the force produced. The greater the force exerted upon the equipment, the greater the resistance the equipment will apply. The benefit to isokinetic training is that the movements are safe and controlled, so it does not cause postworkout muscle soreness. This form of training is not very practical due to the significant cost of the equipment, but will sometimes be found in health clubs or clinical settings.

Benefits of Resistance Training

Your clients will experience many physiological and psychological benefits from resistance training. They will be able to receive important feedback even when you are not present. They can view their chart and see how they have increased the amount of weight they can lift, and look in the mirror and see visible results of their hard work.

Everyone can benefit from resistance training. As people age they lose muscle mass, and the musculoskeletal system itself does not function as effectively. Resistance training can slow and even reverse this loss of bone, muscle, and function. The result is a healthier, more confident individual. Another, often overlooked, benefit to resistance training is that it helps to maintain a normal body weight. Most people assume that cardiovascular activity serves this function. While this is true, resistance training also plays a major role. Other benefits of resistance training include:

- Increased strength
- Muscle hypertrophy (growth)
- Faster metabolism
- Decreased body fat
- Increased self-esteem
- Increased bone density
- Increased speed and power
- Improved body awareness and control

People can be fearful of change, so when it comes to trying new exercises, empower your client through education. Teach him about the exercise and why it will be beneficial. Then demonstrate and, if possible, break the exercise down. Start simple and gradually increase the complexity or difficulty as your client becomes comfortable.

Cardiovascular Training

Cardiovascular, also known as aerobic, conditioning increases strength and efficiency of the heart, lungs, and vascular system in carrying oxygen and nutrients through the body. It will also help your clients lose weight, reduce stress, and increase stamina. During this form of training, the body will break down stored carbohydrates and fats and use them for energy. When an individual expends more calories than he takes in, he will lose weight, and this is one way to assist with that outcome.

Question

Is one form of cardiovascular exercise more beneficial than another?
The best form of exercise will depend on your clients' goals, health, ability level, and preferences. Running will result in faster weight loss than walking, but not everyone will be able to or want to run. Taking all factors into account will uncover the best form of exercise for each individual.

Modes of Cardiovascular Exercise

Cardiovascular exercise can be performed in a variety of settings: at home, in a gym, or outside. It can be anything that brings the heart rate up for an extended period of time. Some common ways to achieve cardiovascular exercise are:

- Walking
- Jogging and running
- Cycling
- Rollerblading
- Swimming
- Cross-country skiing

If your client does not enjoy exercising alone, you can suggest she find a partner or try playing a sport such as basketball, singles tennis, or racquetball. You can also encourage her to try participating in a group exercise class such as spinning, cardio kickboxing, or step aerobics. Some people receive extra motivation and enjoyment from exercising with other people. The more your client likes the program, the better the chances of compliance.

Practical Applications

Some trainers limit themselves strictly to weight training. This approach will diminish the quality of your service. Cardiovascular conditioning is an enormous part of your clients' health and well-being. It will assist in the prevention of many chronic diseases, as well as help your clients reach and maintain a healthy body weight. You can incorporate cardiovascular conditioning into your program in many ways. You may start and end your workouts on a piece of cardio equipment. Or you can request that your clients stay upon completion of your session if given the time. For those clients who train multiple times per week, you can use a portion of each session for cardiovascular exercise.

Essential

Some clients may want to skip the cardiovascular component of your program. In this situation, try to educate the client on the benefits. If you are unsuccessful, you cannot force them to comply. Instead, try to integrate that variable into another part of the program. One way is to incorporate short aerobic intervals in between sets of strength-training exercises.

You will have some clients who are more than willing to perform their cardiovascular conditioning on their own. This is great, but many of your clients simply will not make the time for it. In these cases, continue to encourage them to work on their own while finding creative ways to incorporate cardiovascular training into your appointments.

Cardio Workout Intensity

The next element to consider is the intensity of your cardio workouts. The American College of Sports Medicine (ACSM) has broken down the different levels of intensity into three categories, all based on a percentage of the client's maximum heart rate (MHR):

- Moderate activity is between 55 and 69 percent of MHR
- Vigorous or hard activity is between 70 and 89 percent of MHR
- Very hard activity is 90 percent or more of MHR

To determine the client's maximum heart rate, you can subtract his age from 220. Then take that number and multiply it by the percentage of MHR to figure out what heart rate corresponds to different intensity levels. For example, if he is forty-seven years old, your calculation would look like this:

$$220 - 47 = 173 \text{ MHR}$$
$$173 \times .55 = 95 \text{ beats per minute, the low end of his moderate activity zone}$$
$$173 \times .69 = 119 \text{ beats per minute, the high end of his moderate activity zone}$$

This formula gives you a rough estimate of maximum heart rate, but it won't be entirely accurate, so use these numbers as a guideline only.

Another formula that offers a bit more detail is the Karvonen formula. This formula determines heart rate based on the client's heart-rate reserve (HRR) and a training range that is between 50 percent and 85 percent of his HRR. This all sounds very complicated, but the formula is fairly simple, although you will need to find his resting heart rate (RHR) to use this formula. To find the client's RHR, take his pulse for one full minute after resting quietly for at least thirty minutes:

220 – age = maximum heart rate (MHR)
MHR – resting heart rate (RHR) = heart-rate reserve (HRR)
HRR × 50% or 85% = your training zone %
training zone % + RHR = target heart-rate zone

Here's an example for a thirty-year-old person with a resting heart rate of 60 beats per minute:

$$
\begin{array}{lll}
220 - 30 & = & 190 \\
190 - 60 \ (\text{RHR}) & = & 130 \\
130 \times 65\% & & \\
\quad \text{or } 85\% \ (\text{high end}) & = & 85 - 110 \\
85 + 60 \ (\text{RHR}) & = & 145 \text{ beats per minute} \\
110 + 60 \ (\text{RHR}) & = & 170 \text{ beats per minute} \\
\text{Target heart-rate zone} & = & 145 \text{ to } 170 \text{ beats per minute}
\end{array}
$$

 **Alert**

There's been some speculation in the past few years that the MHR formula, 220 – age, isn't very accurate because the number, 220, is based on a sedentary person. If your client is fit, using that formula may not work for you, and even the Karvonen formula may be a little off.

Now that you have a target heart-rate zone, how do you actually monitor heart rate? One option is by using a heart-rate monitor. A heart-rate monitor is simply a watch that comes with a strap you wrap around the chest during exercise. This strap sends a signal to the watch, allowing the client to see a continuous reading of his heart rate. There are a variety of monitors out there for every budget, from basic models that just measure heart rate, to high-tech models that measure everything from heart rate and calories to pace, speed, and time spent in the zone. You can find heart-rate monitors at most sporting-goods stores and discount stores.

If you don't want to bother with formulas or heart-rate monitors, there are other, simpler, ways to monitor the intensity of your workouts. The simplest method is the talk test. With this test, the client only has to ask himself one question: Am I able to carry on a conversation? If he can talk during his workout without becoming breathless, he's most likely working at a moderate intensity.

Another method to monitor intensity is using a perceived-exertion scale to measure your rate of perceived exertion (RPE). Perceived exertion is simply how hard the client feels he's working during exercise. It's a subjective measure and will differ from person to person, but studies have found that it's an accurate way to monitor exercise intensity. The standard scale most people use is the Borg Scale, which ranges from 6 to 20, 6 being the easiest and 20 being the hardest. Using this scale, 6 would be the equivalent of doing nothing, and 20 would be the client working at his absolute maximum. A moderately intense activity would fall somewhere between 12 and 13.

A simplified perceived-exertion scale can range from 1 to 10:

- **Level 1:** The client feels like he is watching TV and eating bonbons.
- **Level 2:** The client is comfortable and could maintain this pace all day long.
- **Level 3:** The client is still comfortable, but is breathing a bit harder.
- **Level 4:** The client is sweating a little, but feels good and can carry on a conversation effortlessly.
- **Level 5:** The client is just above comfortable, sweating more, but can still talk easily.
- **Level 6:** The client can still talk, but is slightly breathless.
- **Level 7:** The client can still talk, but doesn't really want to. He is sweating profusely.
- **Level 8:** The client can grunt in response to your questions, and can only keep his pace for a short time period.
- **Level 9:** The client feels like he is probably going to die.
- **Level 10:** The client cannot go on.

Using this scale, a moderate pace would be around 4 or 5, while a vigorous pace would fall between 7 and 9.

Cooldown

The cooldown period is probably one of the most overlooked components of the exercise program. You can perform the cooldown in any number of ways. The important thing is that your client is only minimally exerting himself. If utilized properly, the cooldown can provide you with the opportunity to motivate your client and keep her on track. It also gives you the time to present the benefits of continuing to purchase sessions.

Why the Cooldown Is Important

The cooldown allows your client's body to enter homeostasis. Homeostasis is a return to balance. Heart rate will approach normal, and most of the blood that was routed to the muscles will return to the abdomen. It also provides your client with a chance to relish his accomplishments and prepare to move on with his day. If you neglect this portion of the workout, your client may have a more difficult time recovering from the workout physically and mentally.

Using the Time to Educate and Network

The cooldown is a great time to communicate with your client. She is not overly exerting herself and does not need to concentrate as intensely during this portion of the workout. You can discuss her short-term goals and how she feels about her progress. Discuss what you expect her to do for exercise until she sees you next, and help her come up with a game plan so she can complete her assignments. If you have any pertinent information regarding health and fitness, this is a good time to share it. You can also use this opportunity to network. Let your clients know you are looking for referrals, especially if they appear satisfied with the services you are providing.

Stretching

Stretching is used to lengthen muscles, thus allowing the joints to move more freely. While it is commonly believed that stretching should be done both before and after the workout, recent research has caused experts to assert that static stretching should only be done after the workout and dynamic stretching before. Many clients will skip the stretching portion of the workout, so be sure to emphasize the importance of stretching in injury prevention and the reduction of soreness. At the end of each appointment, spend about five minutes stretching your client or instructing him in how to stretch himself. Being flexible and stretching is beneficial because:

- It helps the client relax the muscles he's been working.
- It increases range of motion.
- It helps improve balance and coordination.

- It can help protect the body from injuries during certain activities.
- It feels good and leaves the client feeling more relaxed.

Static Stretching

Static stretching is the form of stretching that will typically come to mind when people are asked to stretch. It involves moving the joint into a position where there is tension on the muscle, and holding that position for approximately thirty seconds.

Essential

You need to show your clients how to stretch safely. Make sure they stretch each muscle group to the point where they feel tension but not pain. Instruct them to hold the stretch for twenty to thirty seconds, and never to bounce. If done incorrectly, stretching can result in muscle spasm or strain.

You may choose to demonstrate the stretches to your client or actually take your client through the movements. If you are considering performing stretches on your client, be sure to obtain their consent beforehand. Not everyone will feel comfortable with this form of contact. The benefit to stretching your client is that you will be able to move the joint further than the client will on his own. Instruct your client to tell you when he feels pressure but not pain.

Dynamic Stretching

Dynamic stretching involves lengthening the muscles through movement. This type of stretching is used during the warm-up and will typically mimic the movements to be performed in the upcoming activity. It helps prepare the muscles and joints for the added stressors of weight training, cardiovascular training, or sports training. This is not to be confused with ballistic stretching, which involves bouncing and can cause tissue damage. These movements are safer and more controlled than ballistic stretching.

Chapter 16

Principles of Programming

There are many factors that will influence the success of your programs. In addition to examining the clients' medical histories and analyzing the results of their testing, you must also look at their lifestyle, and then determine when and how they will exercise. To keep your clients moving forward, you will also need to understand some basic principles of training. By taking all of these factors into consideration, you will be able to address your clients' special needs and create balanced, successful programs.

Principles for Success

There are some basic concepts you must understand in order to create a successful program. These concepts include specificity, overload, and training variables, and are the absolute fundamentals of training. Without utilizing these principles, any attempt to increase strength and conditioning would be ineffective. Even if you are not familiar with these terms, chances are you have applied the principles in your personal exercise program or you would never progress.

Specificity

The premise behind specificity is that you need to stress the system of the body where you want to see benefits. Resistance training will increase muscular strength, but is not an effective way to train balance. Stretching will increase flexibility, but will not affect aerobic conditioning. Specificity is important because, if you are not training the right system, your client may not reach his goals. This is the reason generic, cookie-cutter workouts are unwise and ineffective.

If you have a client who wants to increase upper-body strength, you have to perform upper-body resistance training. Training the legs will make her stronger, but will not help her reach her goal. Strength training for the lower body will likely be a part of the program, but the main focus should be on upper-body strength training, such as bench press, chin-ups, pushups, dips, bicep curls, etc. More specifically, you will need to use enough resistance so she can only perform eight to twelve repetitions. This is where you will truly see strength gains. If she can lift more than twelve, she is training muscular endurance and not muscular strength.

Overload

The principle of overload is that in order to effect a physical change, you must stress the body beyond a certain threshold. This, of course, must still occur within a safe limit. Whether you are training muscular strength, muscular endurance, or cardiovascular endurance, this principle must continuously be applied or your clients will not move toward their goals.

After a period of time, your client's body will adapt to training, and the sixty pounds she was bench pressing will no longer feel like a challenge. To continue seeing progress, you will need to employ the principle of progressive overload. In order to increase chest strength, you will need to increase the weight until she can only achieve eight to ten repetitions. This is a sufficient amount of weight to overload the muscle, resulting in strength gains. If she continues to bench sixty pounds, she will not increase her chest strength. It sounds simple, and it is, but the application of this principle is a key factor in the success of any program.

Training Variables

There are three variables that you can manipulate to keep your clients moving ahead: frequency, intensity, and duration. These variables are exactly what they sound like. Frequency is how often your client performs a certain exercise. Intensity is how hard she works at it, and duration is the length of time she is performing the exercise. You will often have a client who is trying unsuccessfully to lose weight. You might start him out walking on the treadmill three times per week for thirty minutes at three and one-half miles per hour. After several weeks, this will no longer be a challenge to his body. He will need to make a change in the workout in order to progress. You can do this by increasing the number of days he is walking, the speed at which he is walking, or the length of time he is walking. If he does not have more time to devote to exercise, you can increase his speed to three and three-quarter miles per hour. You could also have him perform intervals where he jogs at five miles per hour for one minute, then recovers at his normal pace for three minutes. The same can be true of any of the other components of a program: balance, core strength, muscular strength, muscular endurance, and flexibility. Whatever system needs to be challenged can be overloaded with an increase in frequency, intensity, or duration; small increases are all that is necessary. Remember to keep in mind the fitness level of your client, as well as any limiting factors such as time and personal preferences.

Alert

Your goal is to create a safe, effective, and enjoyable program. Keep in mind that your client may end up performing this on his own. Do not get too complicated or creative with the exercises. If your client finds the program too challenging or confusing, he may become frustrated and lose interest.

Variety Is Key

Without variety in a program, your client will quickly become stagnant and bored. Workouts should not change only in difficulty, but in format as well. There are many variables within a program that may be manipulated, including but not limited to, the number of sets per exercise, repetitions per set, rest periods between sets or exercises, and resistance used.

There are always exceptions to the rule. You may have some clients who like to perform the same workouts at the same intensity all of the time. The routine is comfortable for them and they resist and dislike change. Since your job is to keep your clients safe and happy, then by all means be accommodating. You can make very small changes for these people by varying the order of the exercises or the number of sets. Or you could try to introduce very small changes periodically and see how they respond. You may be able to nudge them out of their comfort zone a bit with gradual modifications.

Start off with basic exercises that are easy to remember and not too difficult to perform. Ease your clients into the workouts. You can always move to more advanced exercises over time. Setting the bar a little low in the beginning will help people feel more competent, and they will have more confidence to perform the workout without you.

Factors to Consider When Planning a Program

Personal trainers develop and implement exercise programs based on their clients' specific needs. You will not be a very successful trainer if you fail to develop individualized programs. Generic, one-size-fits-all programs will not address the specific needs and goals of all of your clients. Considering multiple variables when creating a program will help your clients reach their goals safely, efficiently, and in a timely manner.

Personal Variables

Every client you work with will have a different lifestyle and personality. Some may be workaholics who never sleep; others may be new moms who need some time for themselves. Some clients will be confident and focused and some will not. These factors will impact the design and function of the exercise program:

- **Time:** The time your client can devote to the workout will determine how many exercises you can include.
- **Frequency:** The number of days per week your client can exercise will impact the balance of strength and cardiovascular training.

- **Personal Preference:** If your client does not enjoy the program you put together, she will be much less likely to comply.
- **Goals:** Your clients' goals will impact the focus of your program. The client who wants to lose weight will spend much more time and energy performing cardiovascular exercise than the client who wants to gain muscle.
- **Motivation:** A client who is highly motivated will be willing to work harder and longer than one who is unmotivated.
- **Lifestyle:** Look at where your client is starting and make small, manageable changes in her lifestyle. Anything drastic will not be maintainable.

Physical Variables

Your first priority should be to create a safe program. In order to do this, you must consider your clients' age, health status, and the results of the exercise testing. The client may be taking medications that will impact his response to and tolerance of his program. Or he may be trying to prevent the cardiovascular disease that runs rampant in his family. If your client wishes to run a five-mile road race, but performed poorly on his aerobic testing, you know you have to really work on cardiovascular conditioning. If your client has an old knee injury, you will probably not include squatting in his program. There are so many physical variables that it would be impossible to discuss each one. The main thing is to be aware of them, learn how to handle them, and ask for assistance when necessary.

Special-Needs Populations

At some point you will likely be approached by an individual who has special needs. A person is considered to have special needs if he requires program modification due to factors that put him at a greater risk of injury or adverse health effects. They may have a specific medical condition or simply be in an age group that requires special consideration. If you do choose to work with special-needs clients, it is even more important to have an understanding of their specific needs. Before you agree to take on a client who has special needs, assess whether or not you have the knowledge and ability to develop a safe and effective exercise program.

In today's fitness industry, you have many opportunities to obtain additional certifications or education to work with various populations. Special-needs populations fall under a vast array of categories. Most likely you would choose one or two populations in which to specialize. The following is a list of some of the populations you may encounter:

- Youth
- Baby boomers
- Prenatal and postnatal women
- Postrehabilitation patients
- Patients with chronic diseases such as diabetes
- Cardiac rehabilitation patients
- People suffering from degenerative diseases such as multiple sclerosis
- People who are obese
- People with musculoskeletal limitations
- People with severe asthma

When you are working with these populations, there will be times when you will need assistance from someone who is more qualified. The person you should turn to is the client's doctor or physical therapist. Or in the case of a healthy population, you may speak to a more experienced trainer. Your primary responsibility is the safety and wellness of your clientele.

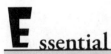

E ssential

If you choose to work with a population that's dealing with medical problems, you must be prepared to work in conjunction with a medical professional such as a doctor or physical therapist. They may give you an exercise prescription, which is simply an exercise program provided by a medical professional.

Baby boomers are, as a group, an increasing part of the special-needs population. They are getting older but wish to maintain an active, fulfilling lifestyle. Because of their age, they will likely have some orthopedic considerations such as injuries or arthritis. They are also at higher risk for heart disease, high blood pressure, and high cholesterol than the middle-aged population. These people have been on this earth for many years, and a great deal can transpire that you will need to consider when making your programs. The program that is suitable for a thirty-year-old will likely not be suitable for a sixty-year-old.

Today's youth are playing organized sports at an earlier age, thus increasing their need for strength and conditioning and increasing their potential for injuries. Not only are they playing earlier, but children are specializing in one sport year-round instead of playing several. This increases the chances of developing muscular imbalances, which ultimately limit joint function. You will need to understand the age of the client and the sport they're participating in, as well as assess physical condition, in order to work with this population.

Program Considerations for Cardiovascular and Resistance Training

For a new trainer, and sometimes even for an experienced trainer, creating a successful program can feel overwhelming. There are so many components and variables to consider. What will it take to help your client progress, while enjoying the process? How do you meet people where they are and help them get where they want to go? As you gain knowledge and experience, you can make your programs more complex, but in the beginning, your best bet is to stick with the fundamentals.

Resistance Training

Everyone needs muscular strength and endurance training. As people age, they lose muscle mass and function. However, your programs will differ depending on the fitness level of your client, as well as his past experiences with weight training. With a beginner you will start with simple, stable exercises using lighter weights and higher repetitions. You might even use mostly machines to build her baseline strength. If your client has been training for years or is an athlete, the exercises will need to be more complex and more difficult in order to increase muscular strength and endurance. For this type of client you would use more functional training as well as heavier weights.

Regardless of the difficulty of the program, order of exercise and proper rest between sets are important, so the muscles can be safely overloaded. Fatiguing the muscles too early in the program will not allow for an efficient workout. Generally, you want to start training the large muscle groups first, then move on to the smaller muscles. If you work the smaller muscles first, you may not be able to train the larger muscles as hard, because the assisting muscles are already fatigued. If you choose to work the larger muscles first, the order of muscles used might look something like this:

- **Chest:** bench press
- **Back:** chin-ups
- **Thighs and Butt:** lunges
- **Shoulders:** overhead press
- **Calves:** calf raises
- **Arms:** bicep curls and triceps dips

You could also choose to train certain muscle groups on certain days, but most of your clients will not have the time to do this type of training; they'll need a full-body workout two to three times per week.

The amount of time you spend on each body part will depend on the client's goals. Some people do not like to do lower-body weight training because they want to keep their legs fresh for their cardiovascular training. For these people, you may spend a few minutes on these areas, but focus more on upper body and core. Other clients will really want to tone their legs and butt, so you will spend more time working those areas. It is fine to focus more effort on a specific area, but try not to neglect any muscle groups. If you do, you can create muscular imbalances that will predispose your clients to injury.

Cardiovascular Training

Your average client should be participating in cardiovascular exercise three to five times per week for twenty minutes to an hour. The intensity will vary depending on age and fitness level, but should generally be between 55 and 80 percent of their maximum heart rate. For a less precise way to tell your clients how hard they should be working, you can instruct them to work hard enough to breathe heavily, but still be able to talk to someone. If the workout is not intense enough, your client will not be improving heart and lung health, and will also not be burning many calories. If your client is highly conditioned or wishes to become highly conditioned, the frequency, intensity, and duration of the exercise will be much greater.

 Fact

For the client who wants to rapidly improve cardiovascular conditioning, interval work is helpful. Intervals are short bursts of increased intensity followed by an active recovery period. Your client may jog at six miles per hour for several minutes, increase to seven and one-half miles per hour for one to two minutes, then return to a six mile per hour jog for several more minutes.

When a client is just beginning a program, you may need to start very slowly and simply. For some people, just walking for ten minutes is a challenge. Take your client where he is comfortable, and create a manageable way for him to progress to where he needs to be. Perhaps he will begin by walking three times per week for ten minutes, then add two minutes per week to each session. In five weeks, he will be walking for twenty minutes, and in ten weeks he will be walking for thirty. If walking is too difficult, the stationary bike is a good place to start. Whatever you choose, remember to consider what your client will enjoy. Many people find cardiovascular exercise to be boring. So encourage your clients to find a buddy and choose a variety of modes of exercise.

Periodization

Periodization, the process of varying a program over specific periods of time, has been shown to be the most effective way to design programs. When done correctly, you will maximize results in less time. A periodized program is made up of three cycles. The first and shortest is a microcycle. A microcycle is planned for anywhere from approximately two to ten days, but is generally about a week. A mesocycle is typically three weeks to three months in duration, and contains numerous microcycles. Finally, a macrocycle is generally about a year, and contains multiple mesocycles. In these cycles, volume and intensity are manipulated in a very specific way. Rest and recovery are planned into the program so as to avoid injury.

Why Periodize Your Programs?

Periodized programs are very individualized for two reasons. First, they take into account personal goals, preferences, and levels of ability. Second, individuals will respond differently to the same program. For this reason, it will be necessary to constantly re-evaluate the program and monitor progress to maximize effectiveness.

Periodization is a complex model of training. Numerous books have been written and a tremendous amount of research performed on this one concept. It is, however, undeniably effective. Therefore it is in the best interests of any trainer to study and learn as much as he can about periodized training. Keep it simple in the beginning, and as you become more proficient and comfortable, you can make your programs more complex. Periodization is a concept, not an exact science, so once you understand the basic ideas, you can start to implement them in your programs.

Breaking Plateaus

No matter how good your program or how hard your clients work, plateaus are an almost unavoidable part of the fitness journey. However, they may be kept to a minimum in both frequency and duration. A plateau occurs when the client is no longer seeing changes and improvements; he is no longer moving toward his goals, but rather remains at a standstill for a period of time. This is frustrating and discouraging, and may occur for a number of reasons.

Why Plateaus Occur

The most common reason for a plateau is failure to vary the program. The body is an amazing machine. Muscles have memory and the body quickly adapts to the demands placed upon it. Therefore, if you perform the same routine the same way for an extended period of time, the body will get used to the stress and the effects will diminish.

You may find a client reaches a plateau due to an orthopedic injury. In this case, the goals of the program need to be rewritten to focus on the rehabilitation of the injury. If you are not qualified in this area, you should refer the client to a physical therapist and work with her to help your client return to full function. Once the injury has been rehabilitated, you can refocus on progressing the client's program.

Plateaus may also occur because a client has reached his genetic capabilities in a certain area. Everyone has a maximum potential and will be unable to progress after a certain point. This, however, is a rare occurrence, but if it does occur you can simply focus on developing another area of fitness.

Plateaus can also be the result of the client underestimating what she is eating. Keeping a food journal can help keep track of any extra calories she may be consuming. Some things for your clients to watch out for include:

- **Liquid calories.** Many people forget to count the beverages they're drinking. For example, drinking a lot of fruit juice or sports drinks can add extra calories, and visiting coffee shops on a regular basis for smoothies and other sweet drinks can pile on more calories than one might think.
- **Alcohol consumption.** This is another area where many clients don't keep track of extra calories. On the average, twelve ounces of light beer can contain more than 100 calories—drink four or five of those in one sitting and they've taken in an extra 400–500 calories.

- **Hidden calories.** Does your client put a lot of cream in their coffee? Does she nibble on snacks throughout the day that she doesn't keep track of? Make sure she writes down every single thing she eats, even if that means counting peanuts or chips, to make sure she is really eating the calories she thinks she is.
- **Measure, measure, measure.** Clients may complain about having to measure their food, but they will be shocked when they actually do it and see how much they're really eating. Have your client measure everything she eats for one week to see if she's on track.
- **Make their own meals.** The only way for your client to really know what's in her food is to make the meal herself. Eating out, even if she chooses healthier options, can lead to eating more calories.

Avoiding or Getting Past a Plateau

It takes foresight and experience to be able to avoid or minimize plateaus. Every trainer has struggled with this issue. In an ideal world, a client will set her goals and gradually move closer until she has attained them. At this point, she will either set bigger goals or work toward maintenance of her previous goals. Things will rarely happen this way. Even a properly developed program can still result in your client reaching a plateau, though a well-planned program will have few plateaus and they will be relatively short in duration. Minimizing the damage caused by a plateau is important. Your client may become frustrated by a plateau and lose her focus. Worse, she may quit because she feels discouraged. The more time your client spends in a plateau, the more likely she will be to lose her motivation.

A beginning client will rarely reach plateaus, but if she does, it is not as difficult to move past as it can be for the advanced client. Varying frequency and intensity are usually enough. However, you will have to employ more advanced techniques for clients who are very fit or are long-time exercisers.

- **Periodization:** See page 210.
- **Forced Reps:** Upon completion of the required repetitions, the client performs two to five more repetitions with the assistance of the trainer.
- **Compound Training/Supersets:** Involves training a muscle group with back-to-back exercises (a dumbbell chest press followed by a pushup).
- **Negative Repetition Training:** The client performs the lowering phase of the exercise, but requires assistance for the pushing phase, because the weight used is too heavy to be lifted without help.

Once again, these are advanced techniques only to be performed by experienced trainers working with experienced clients. Employing them will help your clients stay motivated and continually moving toward their goals.

Cross-Training

Cross-training allows clients to enjoy variety and stimulation while working toward their goals. It can also help them get through a plateau. The basic concept of cross-training involves using different forms of exercise in order to bring balance and variety to a program. It helps prevent overuse injuries, and can also be psychologically stimulating. If, for example, your client is a runner, she could cross-train by swimming or biking once or twice a week. She would still receive cardiovascular benefits, without placing the same types of stress on her muscles and joints. Cross-training is only beneficial if your client enjoys what she is doing. Discuss some options with your client before making any decisions.

Giving Homework

It is simply not enough for a client to work with you once or twice a week. In order for him to reach his goals, he will need to exercise on his own. You are there to help and guide your client, but he must also be able to motivate himself. Educate your client about what he needs to do when he is not with you, and hold him accountable for his assignment.

Get Your Client Involved

While you do need to coach and motivate your client, you do not want to come across as a dictator. Ask for the client's input into what type of exercise they want to do and have time for. If you simply try to dictate what you want her to do without gaining insight into what she is willing and able to do, she will likely not comply with your requests. You want the program to be as manageable and enjoyable as possible, because this will increase the likelihood of success. People do not want to spend five hours per week feeling miserable. Most will look to exercise for enjoyment and stress relief, and if they do not feel this way in the beginning, you need to help them feel this way.

Giving Instructions

Be clear and specific when giving instructions to your client. If you want her to walk on the treadmill twice in the upcoming week, tell her how long and at what speed. Do not assume anything or expect your client to assume anything. You can even go as far as to write down for the client precisely what to do on each day of the week. The more precise your instructions, the less room there will be for confusion. Remember that this may be someone's first time exercising. He might be unsure of himself and what he is capable of doing. If you are not specific in your instructions, your client may push himself too hard or not hard enough. Writing "bicep curls" on his instruction sheet is much different than writing "perform ten repetitions of bicep curls with twenty-pound dumbbells for three sets." Proper communication will be essential. Once you have given your instructions, you might ask your client to explain back to you what you are looking for, or at least answer any questions your client might have. Make it clear that if he tries the program and feels unsure of any component, he should contact you before continuing.

Chapter 17

Motivating Your Clients Through Goal-Setting

There are countless theories and philosophies on motivation. It is a topic that has been discussed and debated for centuries. Extensive research has been performed, and numerous books have been written and workshops given on this topic. No one can debate, however, that without motivation, any exercise program will fail. Your success and longevity in the personal-training business will be due in large part to your ability to keep your clients motivated. Doing so requires a great deal of thought, time, energy, and commitment from both trainer and client.

What Motivates Each Individual

The simple fact is that few people are able to begin and adhere to an exercise program for an extended period of time. For whatever reason, their motivation is simply not strong enough. One of your most difficult and most important tasks as a trainer will be helping your clients stay motivated and on track. Each individual client will be motivated by different factors and circumstances, and you need to discover what those variables are.

Types of Motivation

Motivation has been defined as inspiration, encouragement, stimulation, impetus, or incentive. These are the factors directing goal-oriented behavior, and are generally broken down into two types or forms: intrinsic and extrinsic. Intrinsic motivation comes from within the individual. When someone is intrinsically motivated, they are doing something because they want to do it. The behavior provides them with enjoyment and/or satisfaction. Extrinsic motivation comes from outside influences. Behaviors are exhibited in order to obtain a reward or to avoid punishment. Individuals may have a tendency toward one or the other, but everyone is both intrinsically and extrinsically motivated.

 Fact

Self-monitoring devices such as pedometers, calorie trackers, and heart-rate monitors provide people with concrete feedback and can be great external motivators. They provide an objective means to see how hard someone is working, and a tangible way to measure progress.

Most clients will retain your services because they need to fulfill some physical or emotional need. However, if you ask your clients, "What are your intrinsic motivators, or how can I best extrinsically motivate you," they may look at you like you are crazy. They only know that they want to lose ten pounds so they can fit into a bathing suit or their favorite pair of jeans. You have to figure out what their motivations are, and how to best keep them motivated, by asking the right questions and through trial and error. The simplest way to get started is by asking clients why they came to see you and what they hope to accomplish. Their responses will tell you what their motivations are. By determining what their needs are and the motivation behind them, you will be able to keep your clients on track to fulfill those wishes and needs.

Factors Affecting Motivation

People can accomplish almost anything if they are motivated enough. But what does it take to reach that level of motivation? It starts with a positive, optimistic attitude and a belief system. If a client believes they can do something, they will feel better about themselves, and be more likely to achieve it. If, on the other hand, a client does not come in with the right mindset, you can have a difficult time helping him stay motivated. Other factors that may influence your client's levels of motivation are:

- Past history of exercise
- Whether they are exercising because they want to or because they need to
- Level of support from friends and family
- How much time they have for exercise
- Whether or not they believe they can be successful
- How much they enjoy what they are doing

The client who enjoys exercise, believes she can be successful, and has support from loved ones will be much easier to motivate than the client who was told by her doctor that she must exercise to get her blood pressure down, and hates every minute she is there. You may be able to help her change her attitude, but it will require a significant effort on your part.

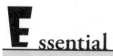

Motivation will fluctuate through the course of a program. In the beginning, your client may need more extrinsic motivation (the desire to lose ten pounds) until exercise becomes a habit and they start enjoying it more. If they are still on a program one year down the line, they are likely motivated by more intrinsic factors, such as self-satisfaction.

Motivation is a team effort. Neither trainer nor client should bear the burden individually. Your job is to believe in your clients and help them believe in themselves. Knowing that you are invested in helping them produce a positive outcome will be a powerful extrinsic motivator.

The Importance of Goal-Setting

Without goals you would not have any clients. People hire you because they want to achieve a certain outcome. Goals give both you and your clients a map to follow toward desired results. They also provide feedback on how well the client is doing and how effective your programs are. Essentially, goals help you see where your clients are going and how well they are progressing toward the desired result. Without them, there is no clear point to work toward, and no direction for the program.

Goals Influence Behavior

Your clients' goals are their driving force to exercise. If you do not set goals with your clients, their commitment to exercise may diminish over time. Goals are very powerful motivators. If your clients set fitness goals, they will be much more likely to do what is necessary to accomplish them. People who set goals are more committed to reaching the desired outcome, and without commitment you will have very little success. Goals increase focus and intensity in both trainer and client.

Alert

When someone truly wishes to achieve a goal, his behavior will reflect this desire. He will demonstrate his commitment by putting his time and energy into making it happen. If your client does not demonstrate commitment, perhaps the goals were improperly written to begin with. Help your client rewrite them so they are more in line with his belief system.

Consider that client who said she wanted to lose ten pounds. Her goals may be to consume 1,500–1,600 calories per day, perform one hour of cardiovascular exercise five times per week, and lift weights twice a week for an hour. She knows exactly what she needs to do and reviews her goals daily. When the alarm sounds at 5 A.M., she will be much more likely to get up and go to the gym than the person who wants to lose ten pounds but has no plan for how to do so.

Emotional Aspects

Setting and achieving goals will boost your clients' confidence and improve their self-esteem. Achieving a goal shows clients that they're making progress and brings about a sense of accomplishment. This is true for the beginning exerciser right up to the professional athlete. The more the client accomplishes, the better they feel, and the more they feel they can accomplish.

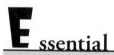

The client with a positive outlook will be easier to keep on track than the client who feels frustrated and negative about what he is trying to accomplish. If you cannot help your client change from a negative to a positive state of mind, he will be unlikely to succeed. Setting and achieving goals is one way to increase positive emotions.

Many of the people who hire you will have experienced past failures and feel unsure of their abilities. You may see the woman who has tried unsuccessfully for fifteen years to lose her "baby weight," or the man who has had to take numerous breaks from exercising because of chronic low-back pain. When you set small, attainable goals for these people and they reach them, they will begin to feel more confident and positive about what they have the potential to accomplish. This will lead to setting bigger goals, but more importantly, it can change their attitude toward exercise. They will begin to look forward to exercising and will make it more of a priority. This will again lead to more successes, and the cycle continues.

Put Goals in Writing

Setting goals is much more effective when you put them in writing. Seeing your goals on paper makes them more real. Have your clients actually do the writing, as this will make them feel even more involved and invested in the process. Keep a copy for yourself in their file so you can reference it when designing programs. This will also help you remember to track their weekly and monthly progress. If your clients will comply, have them keep a copy for themselves on an index card and carry it with them. The more they look at the card throughout the day, the more focused and in tune they will be with achieving their goals.

Long-Term versus Short-Term Goals

Your clients may hire you with one goal in mind, or they may have ten. It is best to limit the number of goals so you can really focus on them. One long-term goal and two to three short-term goals are usually sufficient. You can always add more as the program progresses.

Long-term goals should be challenging enough to require six months to one year to accomplish. For someone who has never exercised before, a long-term goal may be to jog three miles. To make the task feel more manageable, long-term goals are broken down into smaller, short-term goals. Short-term goals may be daily, weekly, or monthly, and provide a way to celebrate smaller successes through the process. Achieving the smaller successes of short-term goals will help give your client the confidence and motivation to achieve the bigger, longer-term goal.

 **Alert**

You, as the trainer, need to help your clients set goals that are challenging but attainable. Your client may want to lose twenty pounds in a month, but that is unhealthy and unrealistic. Have them make a long-term goal of twenty pounds in four months, and a short-term goal of one to two pounds per week.

How to Write Goals

Goals need to be specific, measurable, and achievable. They should also be positive and written in the first person. A goal of losing weight is insufficient. It leaves you with too many questions. How much weight do they want to lose? Is it one pound or one hundred? How long do they have to lose the weight? A month? A year? Have your client specifically state how much weight they want to lose, and a precise date for the completion of the goal. A better way to phrase this goal could be, "I will lose ten pounds by August first." If a client wishes to run a marathon, they may make a goal stating, "I will run this year's New York City Marathon in under four hours." When goals are stated in this manner, as the trainer, you will be better equipped to create the program, because you know precisely what the client wants and what type of time frame you are working within. You will be more focused, and so will your client.

Once the long-term goal has been set, make a plan for how to reach it using short-term goals. Include particulars about how the exercise will be performed. Answering the following questions should ensure adequate detail:

- When will the client exercise: before work, at lunch, after work, or some other time?
- Where will they exercise: at the gym, outside, at home?
- How much exercise will they perform: thirty minutes, an hour?
- How often will they exercise: every day, every other day, five times per week?

Well-written short-term goals might look like this: "I will run outside three times per week before work for three miles. If it is raining, I will run on the treadmill." "I will lift weights twice a week at the gym for forty-five minutes during my lunch. If I cannot get to the gym at lunch, I will go after work." The more detail that is included, the more accountability your clients will have in meeting their goals. Obviously they will not be perfect at it. That is why it is called a goal; it's a work in progress.

If a client's goal is to look a certain way (flat abs, more muscle definition, bigger arms), have them find a picture of what they want to look like and put it on the back of their index card. If they can vividly imagine their success, they will be more motivated and their goals will feel more attainable.

Keeping Your Clients Focused

Your clients want to change, but change is hard. They want to meet their goals, but there are so many ways they can become derailed. Modifying ingrained behaviors is an extremely difficult task. This is why they hire you. You are equipped with the knowledge and tools to get your clients on track and moving in the right direction.

Accountability

Because you will not be with your clients for the majority of the time, you want to help them feel responsible for their own actions and behaviors. You can do this in several ways. Require your clients to keep an exercise journal, so they have to put in writing what type of exercise they performed, along with when, where, and how long they exercised. If your clients set nutritional goals, have them keep a food journal where they record what they are eating and in what amounts. If your client would rather use a computer or handheld device, there are numerous programs and Web sites on the market that can be used for this purpose. Once a week or so, they should bring you the records so you can check their progress. Because no client wants to disappoint their trainer, simply knowing that they will have to show you will make them more likely to perform the desired behaviors.

Tracking Progress

Everyone wants to know how they are doing. That is why keeping records of your clients' progress makes sense. Keeping track of progress will help them see that they're moving toward their goals. Not only will they be interested to see what they have accomplished, but this is also a great motivational tool.

There are numerous ways to keep client records. First, mark down what your client does during each workout on a chart. They can do the same when they workout on their own. This allows them to see increases in the amount of weight they can lift or the number of repetitions they can perform. You can also periodically perform exercise testing and mark it in their chart so they can see how far they've come from the initial appointment, and whether they are on track to meet their goals in the predetermined time frame. It can be something as simple as a pushup test or a timed mile run, as long as the test performed is related in some way to the client's goals. Having your clients write down how they feel about their program and progress once a week will help track their attitudes. They may look back in six months and realize how much confidence they have gained and how much more they enjoy their workouts than when they started.

If your clients will use them, journals are a great way to track progress. Journaling can be done with a pen and notebook or on the computer. There are also some great online tools available, such as the one offered by trainerforce.com, that offer online journals. If you pay for an account with Trainerforce, your clients can log on to your Web site and fill out a workout or nutritional log, then e-mail it to you for your records.

Tracking Baseline Measurements

Tracking a few baseline measurements will help your client see she is moving in the right direction. A basic number to keep track of is your client's body mass index (BMI). This is a calculation based on height and weight. BMI is a general way to see whether your client falls into a healthy weight range. The formula used to calculate BMI is:

$$BMI = (\text{weight in pounds} \div [\text{Height in inches} \times \text{Height in inches}]) \times 703$$

For example, if the client weighs 165 pounds and is 65" tall, you would use the following calculations: $(165 \div [65 \times 65]) \times 703 = 27.4$ BMI.

The following guidelines will help determine how healthy your client's BMI is:

- **Obese:** over 30
- **Overweight:** between 25 and 29.9
- **Healthy:** between 18.5 and 24.9
- **Underweight:** below 18.5

Next up are circumference measurements. Measuring different areas of your client's body is helpful in determining whether she is losing fat or muscle. Muscle is denser than fat, so if she gains muscle from her workouts, that could make the scale go up. But muscle also takes up less space than fat, which means her measurements will go down no matter what the scale says. It's best to measure as many areas as possible, because everyone loses body fat in a different order. At the very least, you'll want to measure around her chest, upper arms, forearms, waist, hips, thighs, and calves. Use the following guidelines when taking the measurements:

- Measure both arms and legs, because there will be differences between the right and left sides of the body.
- For all areas except the waist, measure around the widest or largest part of each area; for the waist, measure around the smallest part, or one-half inch above the navel.
- Hold the tape measure tight, but not so tight that it's digging into the skin.
- Don't let the client "suck it in" while measuring.
- Have the client wear the same clothes each time you measure.

E ssential

You might find online calculators helpful for getting some of your baseline measurements. For example, the Body Mass Index (BMI) Calculator (✎http://about.com/exercise/bmicalc) does the work for you. Just plug in your client's weight in pounds and his height in inches and you'll get his BMI, along with information about whether the client is considered underweight, healthy, overweight, or obese.

Tracking the client's body-fat percentage is also helpful. This will allow you to make sure your client is losing fat and not muscle. There are a number of ways to test body fat, some more accessible than others. The most accurate and the least accessible are hydrostatic weighing and DEXA (a kind of body scan). Another option is to measure your client's body fat using calipers (fondly known as the "pinch test") to measure different areas of her body to calculate body fat. The accuracy of calipers largely depends on the tester, so you'll want to learn this skill from an experienced colleague.

Whichever test you choose, you can use the following table to get an idea of different categories of body fat for men and women:

Body-Fat Percentages*		
Categories	Women	Men
Essential Fat	10–12%	2–4%
Athletes	14–20%	6–13%
Fitness	21–24%	14–17%
Acceptable	25–31%	18–25%
Obese	32% plus	25% plus

*From the American Council on Exercise (ACE)

To make things easy, use the following form to record your client's weight, BMI, body fat, and measurements. Take her measurements every four weeks or so to see how she's doing. Try to avoid taking them every day or even every week, because these numbers don't show small, incremental changes the client's body is making, and that may discourage her, even though the changes are happening.

Progress Chart   Date:

Weight		Height	
Body fat		Body mass index (BMI)	

Circumference Measurements

Forearm (R/L)		Upper arm (R/L)	
Chest		Waist	
Hips		Thighs (R/L)	
Calves (R/L)			

Keeping track of where your client is and how far she's come is just one way to keep her motivated and on the right track. Remember that the accuracy of body-fat tests can vary widely depending on the test and the circumstances. Instead of focusing on that, have the client look at these numbers as her starting place. As long as the numbers keep going down, the client will know she's on the right track.

 Fact

Web sites like *trainerforce.com* are a nice resource for both you and your clients. For a monthly fee, you can use this site to create programs and give your clients a password so they can access the site. You could charge your clients a small additional fee for this service to cover your costs, or simply write off the expense.

There will be times when your clients feel frustrated and overwhelmed. During these times, it is helpful to review their past successes. This is much easier to do if you have kept accurate, thorough records.

Giving Feedback and Encouragement

What you are asking your clients to do is not easy. You are challenging them physically, mentally, and emotionally. You are pushing them to their limit and are asking them to push themselves as well. Your clients need your praise and encouragement for their efforts and achievements. They want to please you, and look to you for approval and support, especially if they are not receiving it from anyone else. Sometimes a simple "you can do this" is enough, and other times you will need to put forth more effort. For the client who you can see is struggling, you could send a supportive note or e-mail. If they leave their exercise logs at the gym, periodically put a note on them with a nice quote or a kind word. Be creative and thoughtful. The extra effort will be appreciated and is much needed.

Sometimes your clients will do well and sometimes they will not. It is not your job to berate or degrade. The client will beat himself up enough for the both of you. Even when he may be failing miserably, you must always maintain an upbeat, positive attitude.

Recognizing and Rewarding Success

With all of the emphasis on motivating and encouraging clients, you may think trainers more closely resemble psychologists or cheerleaders than coaches. But neglecting to recognize your clients' achievements is a mistake. Rewards and recognition are huge motivators of behavior. They increase clients' positive feelings about exercising and about themselves. Giving rewards may feel silly or juvenile, but it is simply a proven way to increase success.

Rewards Are Important

Rewards reinforce positive behaviors and are essential to long-term success. They give your clients a sense of accomplishment and elicit positive feelings. While meeting a goal is a reward in itself, it may not be enough of a motivator.

Part of your goal setting can involve attaching a small reward to the accomplishment of each short-term goal, and a major reward for the accomplishment of the long-term goal. This will provide your clients with additional motivation, and will give them something to look forward to.

What Constitutes a Reward?

There are two types of rewards: tangible and intangible. Tangible rewards are concrete, such as a new pair of shoes. Your client can physically hold or have this type of reward. Giving a client a T-shirt for training consistently for six months is a tangible reward. Intangible rewards cannot physically be touched, such as praise or a trip to the movies.

You need to be giving your clients intangible rewards on a regular basis by verbally acknowledging their successes. Look for reasons to recognize achievements. Has your client been consistently sticking to their nutritional plan, put in extra time on the treadmill, improved their core strength? If so, tell him how proud you are and what a great job he is doing. It is not necessary to give your clients intangible rewards, though if you choose to it will certainly be appreciated.

Your clients also need to reward themselves for a job well done. Specific rewards will depend on what the client likes and can afford. Advise your clients to stay away from food as a reward or anything else that may sabotage their efforts. Depending on their budget, they may choose something like new clothes in a smaller size, a show or concert, or new roller blades.

There will be times when friends and family should not be part of a client's support system. They may feel apprehensive and resistant to the changes your client wishes to make, and will therefore sabotage rather than encourage their efforts. Before designating a support system, discuss this possibility, and if necessary, find alternative means of support.

Keys to Success

While there is certainly no fail-proof system, there are ways you can help safeguard your client against failure and disappointment. Commitment, support, and a good plan are key factors for success. You and your clients working together can find the system that will be effective for them as individuals.

Commitment

If your clients are going to successfully achieve their goals, they need to be 100 percent committed to doing what it takes to get there. As their trainer, you need to be 100 percent behind them, providing them with support and the tools they need to achieve success. If one or both parties are not totally committed, this system will not work. You can show your clients that you are dedicated to their success by providing them with the best possible service. They will demonstrate their dedication through adherence to your program.

The longer you work as a trainer, the easier it will be to assess which clients have the commitment level and those who will need an extra push. Bear in mind that you will not be able to help everyone. If they are unwilling or unable to take the steps you outline for them, your hands are tied. You can provide guidance, support, and encouragement, but you cannot do the work for them.

Establish a Support System

Your clients will likely need more support than you alone can give. You do not have the luxury of tending to them twenty-four hours a day. Encourage clients to set up a support system to help them stay on track with lifestyle changes. Friends and family are a great place to start if they are willing to help with the process.

Instruct your client to be specific with what she needs from her loved ones. Support can take many forms. She may need something simple like verbal encouragement or someone to call if she feels like eating to relieve stress. Maybe she wants a friend to walk with her or to watch her children while she goes for a run.

Professionals can be a part of the support system as well. Depending on your clients' needs and goals, they may use the services of a life coach, counselor, dietician, running coach, or even a religious leader. There are also support groups that address just about every need and situation. Figure out with your clients what they feel comfortable with, but they should have someone to help them besides you. Very few people can do it alone.

Dealing with Setbacks

There will inevitably be times when progress slows, stops, or even moves in reverse. You are working with human beings, not machines. If this does happen, re-examine the client's goals, and if necessary, rewrite them. Perhaps they were too ambitious, and cannot dedicate as much time as they thought they could to their program. Figure out what is getting in the way. Is it fear, stress, fatigue, lack of motivation? You may need to modify their program, or completely rewrite it. The client may simply need to take a break and regroup. Whatever happens, stay positive and try not to let your clients give up and quit.

Chapter 18

Maximizing Client Retention and Satisfaction

There are countless reasons people give for quitting an exercise regimen. They may claim to be too busy, too tired, or even too old. The real problem is that if people do not see the results they desire, they will become frustrated. As a trainer, your job is to help your clients reach their goals in a safe and enjoyable manner. If your clients do not enjoy you and your programs, they will not continue to train with you. In order to keep your clients happy, safe, and moving toward their goals, you will need good communication, as well as variety in your workouts.

Maintaining a High Client-Retention Rate

Client retention is critical to your long-term financial success. It will cost more money and take more time to find a new client than to retain an existing client. Take special care of your current client base, so they will continue to provide you with financial stability.

E ssential

When you explain to potential clients that your current clients have stayed with you for long periods of time, they will draw positive conclusions. On the other hand, if you have a high turnover rate, you are either not running your business properly or are an ineffective trainer.

Retaining your clients is not only profitable, it's also a great selling point for your business. It shows that your current clients are satisfied with you, and that you are providing good customer service. People would not continue with you long term if they were not pleased with you.

As in most businesses, a small percentage of your customers will provide you with the majority of your business. For example, take a trainer who performs an average of thirty sessions per week. Twenty-four of these appointments are spent with ten long-term clients who train two to three times per week. That means 80 percent of his revenue is produced by only a few people. Most personal-training businesses work this way. It is wise to give these core clients a little extra attention, as they are the reason you stay in business.

How Can I Retain My Clients?

Making your clients feel special is a sure way to keep them. A good trainer will make people feel like they are getting their money's worth. A great trainer makes their clients feel like they are getting more than they paid for. There are many ways to accomplish this. After an initial appointment, send out a thank-you card and let your new client know how much you enjoyed working with them and that you look forward to working with them in the future.

E ssential

During the hour you are training, focus on your clients intensely. That hour is theirs, and should feel special. If a client needs to reschedule an appointment, go out of your way to fit them into your schedule, even if it means working a longer day than you expected. It will be greatly appreciated.

You can also make a note of your clients' birthdays and send a card so they know you remembered. Another nice touch is to send weekly mass e-mails to your clients with motivational quotes, interesting facts, nutritional ideas, etc. If you have a client going through a particularly tough time, send them an individual note or e-mail letting them know you are thinking of them. Finally, give your clients something with your company name on it, such as T-shirts, water bottles, or workout towels. Everyone enjoys receiving free gifts, especially if they are useful. The little extras go a long way, and good customer service is more than a little extra. It is everything. If your clients feel you are loyal to them, they will be loyal to you.

 Fact

The longer and more frequently a client trains with you, the greater the likelihood that they will continue with you for the long term. People are creatures of habit, and working with a trainer can easily become a habit for people. This is a very profitable tendency to encourage.

Client Loss

Even the most successful trainers lose clients. It is part of doing business. Many times the loss is a result of situations beyond their control. Focus your efforts on minimizing the number of clients who do not rebook appointments, and on proper management of the losses that do occur.

Do Not Lose That Client

There will always be some people who come and go, but if you are losing a large number of clients, you need to figure out the reason so you can fix the problem. First and foremost, you must make sure you are behaving in a professional manner. Unprofessional conduct will detract from the perceived value of your services and can drive people away. Show up on time for your appointments and be focused and prepared. Also, be sure you are delivering what you promised and what your clients want. If the clients' expectations are not being met, they will become frustrated and quit or find a trainer who will meet their expectations.

How to Handle Client Loss

Losing clients is not only a blow to your wallet, it can feel like a personal failure. If someone chooses to stop buying your services, do not take it personally. This can be difficult, because trainers tend to have close relationships with their clients. A great deal is shared during sessions, and sometimes the professional lines between trainer and client get fuzzy and move toward friendship. Despite this, it is still business. People are spending their hard-earned money on your services, and sometimes circumstances change and they become unable or unwilling to continue.

E ssential

The only way to know for sure if your clients are satisfied is to ask. If you do not feel comfortable asking your clients directly, hand out a survey to be filled out anonymously. Find out what people like best and least about you and your work. Then you can focus on emphasizing the positive and changing the negative.

It is important to determine why a client is no longer working with you. In some cases, it will be a simple issue of time or money and has nothing to do with you at all. Be aware, however, that these may be easy excuses to give, when in fact the person is dissatisfied for some reason. When someone does decide to stop working with you, send them a thank-you note. You may also consider including a satisfaction survey with a prestamped return envelope. The feedback you receive may not help you regain lost clients, but it could help you prevent further loss. Finally, if your client did leave on good terms and simply no longer needs your services, they may be willing to send you referrals. It never hurts to ask.

Exercise + Fun + Results = Satisfaction

Very few people will pay $50 or more for an hour of boredom and drudgery. If they are willing to do so, it likely will not be for very long.

Your clients not only hire you for your knowledge of fitness, but to enjoy themselves. They want to forget the troubles of the day for an hour. Therefore, one major focus in program development should be making it enjoyable for the client. This will mean something different to everyone, which is why the better you know your clients, the more likely it is that you will keep them.

Know Your Clients and Deliver Satisfaction

Every client wants and needs something different from you. Some of your clients will wish to be pushed to their limit. The more closely you resemble a drill sergeant, the happier they will be. These people want to exercise until they are completely spent. If they are still standing after a workout, they will feel they haven't done anything. On the opposite end of the spectrum are the people who want you to coddle them and hold their hands. They may not like to sweat or breathe too heavily. Perhaps this is the first time in their lives they are exercising. If you design the same workout for both types of clients, one or both groups will be disappointed and unsatisfied. There is a good chance they will fire you as their trainer. These are extreme examples, and the majority of your clients will fall somewhere in between these two stereotypes. However, with every client you must determine what they want from you and provide them with it.

Exercise is a science, and when properly applied, it gives results. However, each person is unique, and the key is to discover what will bring success for each individual. The best way to obtain this information is by interview and questionnaire. Your instincts will also play a role, as will experience and commonsense. During your initial consultation, make sure you ask in-depth, open-ended questions. The more information you have, the better equipped you will be to design a program that yields results. When a client sees results, they feel good about themselves. When they feel good about themselves, they are happy, and happy customers are long-term customers. On the other hand, if your client is not satisfied, she probably won't tell you. She will stop working with you and tell other people that she was dissatisfied with your services. In that case, you lose a current client and countless other potential clients.

Bells and Whistles

You will soon realize that after a while your clients will become bored with the same old exercises. Boredom can lead to cancellations, which lead to loss of revenue. The bottom line is, a bench press is a bench press. It is a trainer's job to make traditional exercises interesting and fun by teaching different ways to perform them. The more new and exciting you can make your workouts, the happier your clients will be. If you can keep your clients excited, then you will keep your clients.

E ssential

While seemingly irrelevant, it is quite important to find out what hobbies your clients have. This may give you insight into the type of person they are and what kind of program they will enjoy. Someone who likes mountain climbing and skydiving will want and need a different type of workout than the seventy-year-old golfer.

Nothing is more fun than toys. And there is a constant stream of new gadgets and gizmos for exercise. Some are really innovative, but most are just a new twist on an old idea. Regardless, they are unarguably entertaining. Props can keep your workouts fresh and make them more interactive. There are countless ways to work a client with medicine and stability balls. They are adaptable to all ages and fitness levels, as are numerous other things such as bands, balance pads, and agility ladders. These forms of equipment can keep you more involved in the workout as you hold bands or throw and catch balls. It is something more than simply spotting an exercise or counting a set; your clients will appreciate your increased involvement and will enjoy their workouts that much more.

Client Burnout

Over time, you may find clients suffering from burnout. They begin to lose the motivation to exercise, and eventually you lose them. It may be permanently or just for a period of weeks or months. This is not only discouraging for the client, it is also bad for business. Remember that when you are training a client, other members are watching. People can see when you start working with someone new and when you stop training a client. If you are losing more clients than you are retaining, people will notice and it can negatively impact your reputation.

 Fact

Overuse injuries are slow-onset, nagging injuries that get progressively worse over time. They are also referred to as repetitive-stress injuries, because they are caused by repetitive motions. Common overuse injuries are tendonitis, bursitis, and shin splints. Performing the same motions excessively tends to cause these types of problems.

Signs and Symptoms of Burnout

Burnout can manifest itself in many ways. One major indication is a significant increase in cancellations by a client who has been very consistent in the past. Many times people do not realize they are getting burned out. They may feel overwhelmed or unmotivated, and the only way they know how to deal with it is to cancel their appointments. Your client may also feel bad or be afraid to tell you they need a break. Pay close attention if your clients start exhibiting any of the following:

- Overuse injuries
- Changes in sleep patterns or appearing overly tired
- Dramatic changes in appetite
- Emotional changes such as agitation or depression
- Being unable to complete their usual workout
- Unusual increase in the number of cancellations

These will likely be your first indications that your client may be suffering from burnout. Your job is to watch for signals and have a plan to recognize and overcome burnout so you do not lose people.

Discovering How and Why Your Client Is Burning Out

Once you have recognized that your client is presenting signs of burnout, you need to get to the root cause. Burnout can occur for a number of reasons, though the primary reason is overtraining. Overtraining is a result of inadequate rest and/or lack of variety in the program.

In order to figure out why your client is burning out, you must examine not only the overall training program, but how they are spending the rest of their days. Consider the type and intensity of the exercise they are performing, both with you and outside of the gym. Also take into account what they are doing for work, and what is currently going on in their lives. If your clients are overly stressed in other areas of their lives, they will be more susceptible to burnout.

When you begin to suspect a client is starting down this path, ask lots of questions. The more you can get them to open up, the better the chances you will be able to help them. If the problem has more to do with their personal lives than their workout program, you can still be of assistance. Helping them become aware of the cause is the first step in finding a solution. They may need to get more sleep, address a problem at work, or try some other forms of exercise. Once the cause is determined, the ball is in their court. They may choose to handle it on their own or seek the help of another professional such as a counselor.

Preventing and Recovering from Burnout

Your plan of action for preventing burnout should be threefold: educate, create, and motivate. First, educate your clients about burnout before it happens. Explain that exercise has health benefits, but it is possible to get too much of a good thing. Address the concept of training intensity, and teach them how to push hard enough to effect physical changes without causing too much stress on the body. Emphasize that without adequate rest and proper nutrition, problems can arise. Education is the best defense against burnout and the resulting loss of business. Second, create a sound exercise regimen that continuously evolves so your clients are not performing the same routines repetitively. If your clients are receptive, give them a complete program to follow including weight training, cardiovascular, and any other activities they enjoy, such as Pilates or yoga. Be sure to schedule time for rest and recovery so they do not overdo it. Third, motivate your clients with goal-setting. This will help keep them working toward something and reduce the chances of boredom. Using manageable time frames can minimize frustration and prevent people from trying to accomplish too much too quickly.

E ssential

Fun, excitement, and diversity are keys to keeping your client on the path to success. Cross-training is a great way to keep things fresh and new. Cross-training simply means choosing a variety of exercise methods and techniques. If a client enjoys running, they may choose to cross-train by swimming one or two days per week to minimize stress on the joints.

Client burnout is difficult to recover from. The earlier you catch it, the easier it is to fix. A good place to start is by addressing sleep patterns. Eight hours of sound sleep is the average needed by most adults. You need to examine and modify goals, and may need to rewrite the exercise program. If injuries are a factor, you can reduce exercise frequency and intensity. Other professionals such as doctors, massage therapists, chiropractors, physical therapists, social workers, life coaches, and acupuncturists can be helpful additional resources if you feel the issues are beyond your scope.

Common Mistakes

Imperfection is part of being human, and making mistakes is an inevitable part of the learning process. In the personal-training business, minor mistakes should be considered learning experiences; they will help you grow and improve your skills. Major mistakes in this business can cause you to lose or even injure a client. This type of mistake should be avoided at all costs, as they can result in a bad reputation, decreased productivity, or a lawsuit, and will jeopardize your career.

Pushing Too Hard or Not Hard Enough

Figuring out how to move your clients toward success without overwhelming or discouraging them is a difficult balancing act. Pushing your clients too hard could cause them to become disheartened. Not pushing hard enough could cause them to lose interest. Either way they are dissatisfied, and may choose not to come back. You can avoid these situations by knowing your clients. What are they capable of now? What do they want to achieve? Can they handle an aggressive workout or do they need something milder? What type of workouts do they enjoy? Communication is the key to determining how your clients feel. Ask if they are working too hard or if they want to be pushed harder. You may think you can tell by looking, but people are very good at disguising their discomfort.

Start your clients off slowly until you have a grip on what they can tolerate. You can always make your workouts harder if your client wishes to be pushed more. If you push too hard in the beginning, you may scare your clients away; they may never return for a second appointment.

Lack of Planning and Direction

Failing to adequately plan your clients' workouts is a huge mistake. If you want to maximize results and client satisfaction, you cannot walk into the gym unprepared and create off-the-cuff workouts. You need to do your homework. Your exercise programs should be designed with careful consideration and planning. Take into account the results of pretesting and what it says about the clients' fitness level. That is your starting point. Then consider the clients' goals.

They are your ending point. The question you must answer is: what will get this client from point A to point B in the most efficient way?

Making the Clients' Successes and Failures Your Own

New trainers are especially susceptible to thinking that if a client is not having success, they, the trainer, are to blame. This is generally not the case. You can create the most effective workout and nutritional plans possible, but you cannot make your clients follow them. Very few people will follow your instructions the way they should. As much as you want to do it for them, you can't. You are spending only a few hours a week with your clients, and they can very easily undo the good you are doing during the 165 hours you are not with them.

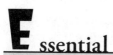

E ssential

If a client cancels without rescheduling, you are losing revenue. This can quickly add up to a significant amount of money. If you charge $50 per session and have four cancellations per week for a month, you will have lost $800. Unless money is not an issue for you, do whatever you can to limit cancelled appointments.

Recapturing Lost Revenue

As you become more established and settled in your business, you will come to rely upon the income from a certain number of appointments in a week. Some weeks there will be a few more or a few less, but ideally it will average out. In order for this balance to occur, you must know how to handle cancellations.

Your Clients Have the Best Intentions

Your clients want to maintain an exercise program. That is why they sought you out and hired you. Unfortunately, people have limited amounts of time. Their schedules are filled with family, work, and social events. Sometimes clients make the commitment to exercise without fully realizing how much of a commitment it really is. If you want to keep your revenues stable, you must help them keep their commitment to you, and make them accountable for cancellations.

You will hear all types of explanations for why a client can not make an appointment: I'm stressed out at work; I have to drop my daughter off at dance; my schedule is full; and so on. While it is important to show empathy and understanding, you also have to consider the lost revenue due to the cancelled appointment.

E ssential

Make your cancellation policy clear from the get-go. Put it in writing and have your clients sign it at their first appointment. Explain that this is your livelihood and you rely on your appointments. If they do cancel at the last minute, they will not be able to argue that they did not know about the policy.

If a client calls to cancel an appointment, be prepared to offer a solution. First, find out the reason they cannot make the scheduled appointment. Then, do everything you can to fit them in another time slot during the week. Inquire about what would work best for the client and try to be accommodating. You may have some clients with more flexible schedules who would be willing to switch their time slot so you can fit in your busier clients. Exhaust all options. You may even offer them a half-hour or forty-five-minute workout if they do not have time for a full hour, and then price the session accordingly. While you want to encourage your clients to keep their appointments with you, do not push them too hard. You do not want to add to their stress levels. Do your best to work with the situation, but if rescheduling is too difficult, let it go.

Time to Pay Up

If a client cancels at the last minute, you need to charge them for the appointment. This may be uncomfortable for you, but it is necessary. You are losing money, and without twenty-four-hours notice, it is difficult to fill an empty time slot. The amount you charge will depend on your predetermined policy. Some trainers charge the entire amount and others only charge a percentage. Asking clients to pay for time they missed is not easy, but you must make a living and your time is valuable. To minimize conflict, be sure that your policy has been clearly stated ahead of time and is understood.

There are, of course, exceptions to this rule. Sometimes people have emergencies or become ill overnight. They may have to tend to a sick child or their car may have broken down. These things happen, and it is up to your discretion whether you choose to charge for the missed appointment. Sometimes it is better for client-trainer relations to let a last-minute cancellation go once in a while. But if it becomes a habit, it needs to be addressed.

Chapter 19

Continuing Education

Obtaining a respectable personal-training certification requires a significant amount of hard work and dedication. However, this is only the beginning. Any credible certifying body requires its members to obtain a certain amount of continuing education in order to maintain that certification. Requirements may be fulfilled by attending seminars, taking home study or college courses, and in some cases by having your work published or speaking at a conference. While it may seem at first to be a hardship because of the time and money involved, continuing education is vital to you as a trainer and to the profession as a whole.

The Need for Continuing Education

Continuing education is important for a variety of reasons. The most obvious is to improve your knowledge base and keep up with new fitness trends. The fitness industry is constantly changing and growing. As new research is performed, ideas and philosophies are modified, or even changed completely. Training techniques considered cutting-edge one year may be outdated the next. By keeping your knowledge current and up to date, you will better serve your clients and run a more successful business.

Credibility for the Profession

There is another very important reason to acquire continuing education. The industry is still largely unregulated; there are no universal guidelines for becoming or remaining a personal trainer. As a result, the level of respect for personal trainers is not always high, especially among health professionals. In order to improve credibility, it is important for trainers to obtain as much education as possible in as many areas as possible. The more knowledgeable trainers are as a group, the more respected they will be as professionals.

Self-Improvement and Professional Development

No trainer knows it all. Everyone has areas in which they are weak or feel unsure of themselves. For example, if you do not have an extensive nutrition background, you may not feel comfortable addressing this aspect of health and fitness with your clients. To help you serve your clients better, you could take a college-level nutrition course, a home-study course, or even a seminar related to nutrition and exercise. This will help strengthen your skills, boost your confidence, and improve the services you provide to your clients. Obtaining CEUs (Continuing Education Units) is a great way to develop the skill sets and knowledge bases where you do not excel.

The knowledge base required to obtain a personal-training certificate is fairly general. As you establish yourself in the profession, you may find yourself wanting to specialize in an area that you really enjoy, such as weight loss, sports performance, or kids' fitness. Continuing education is an ideal way to accomplish this objective.

Becoming Recertified

Each organization has its own requirements to maintain certification. Typically, a recertification period is between two and three years. During that time, members must obtain anywhere from sixteen to sixty hours of continuing education. The major differences between certifying agencies are the number of units they require and what they allow to count toward those requirements. The chosen means of obtaining the continuing education must be preapproved by the organization to ensure the credits are applicable to the profession and meet a certain standard of quality.

The Recertification Process

Across the board, a requirement of recertification is the maintenance of CPR (cardiopulmonary resuscitation) certification through the American Heart Association, American Red Cross, or other approved organization. This is essential in case a client experiences a cardiac emergency during a session. More advanced emergency certifications are not required, but may count toward CEUs, and will also make you better equipped to handle emergency situations.

Upon completion of any type of continuing education, you will be given some form of certificate to verify your participation and act as a record of attendance. Keep all records together in a file in case you are audited and need proof that you did what you reported. At the end of the two or three year period, you will be required to pay a recertification fee and submit a form to your certifying agency specifying how you fulfilled your requirements. They will then send you your new certificate along with the requirements for the next reporting period.

Alert

Regardless of your education or how long you have been a trainer, there is always room for growth and learning. Failure to maintain your certification is irresponsible and demonstrates a careless, unprofessional attitude. It will also result in your being more vulnerable to lawsuits, as you will not be able to maintain your liability insurance.

Obtaining Additional or Advanced Certifications

If you are truly interested in bettering yourself through education, you might consider obtaining additional certifications or earning an advanced certification. In addition to demonstrating professionalism and responsibility, it may also increase your job opportunities, improve your marketability, and allow you to justify charging more for your services. If you have a basic personal-training certificate, you may decide you want to specialize in a certain area such as nutrition. ACE offers a home-study course called Lifestyle and Weight Management Consultant Certification that teaches certified trainers to develop and implement weight-management programs. If you have a degree in a health-related field, you could seek an advanced certification. The ACSM offers a Health/Fitness Instructor certification for "leaders of preventive health programs in corporate, commercial, and community settings aimed at low- to moderate-risk individuals or persons with controlled diseases, such as hypertension, obesity or asthma." These are only two examples. If you would like to investigate your options more thoroughly, log on to the Web sites listed in Chapter 1 or Appendix C. Whatever additional certifications you choose to earn will not only help you earn CEUs, they will increase your knowledge base and improve your qualifications.

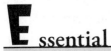

In order to minimize lost revenue, try to attend seminars during times when you know you will not be as busy. Business is usually slower around the holidays and school vacations. Another option is to attend on a weekend. If the seminar you wish to go to requires extensive travel, consider making the beginning or end of your trip a vacation.

Attending Seminars and Workshops

Attending seminars and workshops can be an interesting and enjoyable way to gain hands-on experience. They are the most interactive means by which to obtain CEUs, but can also be the most expensive. There are sometimes travel costs involved, as well as the loss of income from taking time out of work. If you choose to go this route, you want to find the best seminars and learn as much as you can while you're there.

Choosing Which Seminar to Attend

There is nothing worse than spending the money and taking the time out of work to attend a seminar, only to have it fall short of meeting your needs or expectations. This is both frustrating and discouraging. In order to avoid this scenario, be sure to do some research on the people giving the seminar as well as the content. Speaking to someone who attended in the past may help you decide if the course is for you.

Consider the relevance of the subject matter. Will you be able to use the information being offered? Level of difficulty is also an issue. Some seminars are directed at entry-level personal trainers, while others are intended for a more experienced audience. If the course listing does not state who the seminar is geared toward, contact the provider and ask. You do not want to be bored and unchallenged, nor in over your head.

Alert

Remember that you are a professional, and conduct yourself accordingly. This is not a college course, where you can roll out of bed bleary-eyed and show up in your pajamas and a baseball cap. Show up alert, properly attired, and on your game. You will be surrounded by your colleagues, and the last thing you want to do is embarrass yourself.

Finances will also be a factor in whether or not you sign up for a seminar. Only you can determine if the value of the knowledge and the number of CEUs you will receive outweighs what you will pay to attend. Some seminars cost hundreds of dollars and last for several days, while you may find one-day workshops for less than $100. If you are self-employed, these costs, along with travel expenses, may be used as tax write-offs, so make sure you keep your receipts. If you are employed by a club, your employer may pay a portion or all of the costs, but could also dictate what you attend.

Getting the Most Out of Your Experience

The first step to getting the most out of your experience is to arrive well-rested and prepared to learn. A good seminar will always have worksheets and information to take home, but you should still be taking your own notes. You will understand and remember the information more completely if you put it in your own words. Bring a notebook and pen, and sit toward the front so you can ask questions. As you are listening, think of practical ways to incorporate your newfound knowledge in your daily practice, and make detailed notes. For example, if you have a client who has been suffering with low-back pain, and you learn some exercises that will help him, make a note to yourself to add them to the client's program. You will be bombarded with a great deal of new information, and the more specific you can be in your note taking, the more you will remember and be able to apply to your newfound knowledge.

If there is a hands-on section of the workshop, participate as much as possible. You may learn new exercise techniques, verbal cuing, proper spotting techniques, etc. You will remember much more by doing it than you will by simply sitting back and watching. This is also the best way to figure out if you really understand and can perform the task. Plus, if you do have questions, the instructor is available to answer them. If you wait until you are home or at work and find you need more information, you will be out of luck.

Whatever you do learn, practice it as soon as you get back so you don't forget. Sharing your newfound knowledge with a colleague is also a great way to make it stay in your memory.

In-Home Learning

In-home learning is basically any continuing education that takes place on your own. This may include home-study courses, books, magazines, journals, videos, and DVDs. Benefits of in-home learning are that it is less expensive than attending a seminar, and you can take your time reviewing the materials until you feel you understand it. Home-study materials also make great references when you need to look up information for a client or a program.

Home-Study Courses

There are two types of home-study courses: correspondence courses and online courses. They are similar in content, but the style is slightly different. An online course is done completely on the computer, whereas with a correspondence course you may be sent one or all of the following: textbooks, videos, or CD-ROMs. Once you learn the information, you will take an exam either online or by mail, and upon passing will receive a certificate verifying completion of the course. Occasionally, you will have the benefit of an instructor, but this is not common. Overall, for people who are self-motivated, home-study courses are a convenient way to obtain CEUs. You can work on them at your leisure, though they will sometimes need to be completed within a certain time frame. They also tend to be cheaper than seminars and do not involve travel.

Professional Publications

Many organizations publish magazines and journals at little or no cost to their members. These publications allow readers to keep up with the latest research and trends, see new products, and maintain a sense of the industry as a whole. Most of the certifying agencies have their own publications and include them in the cost of membership.

E ssential

If your certifying association offers a journal, it may contain quizzes you can submit for CEUs. There are usually between ten and twenty questions pertaining to a specified article that you can answer and submit online or by mail. The fees for these quizzes are nominal, making them a great way to increase your CEUs.

Trade journals such as *Personal Fitness Professional* and *Club Solutions Magazine* will keep you abreast of new information disseminated through the industry. You can use this information to share with clients, get new ideas on running your business, and to help you think outside of the box. The success stories shared in these publications can be an inspiration to any trainer who dreams of doing great things. Human nature causes people to get stuck in mental ruts, and this constant stream of new ideas can help avoid this pitfall.

Books, Videos, and CD-ROMs

Books, videos, and CD-ROMs offer the opportunity to learn new techniques, strengthen your weaker areas, and focus on a specialty. Their costs are relatively low compared to workshops and home-study courses, and they can be much more specialized and specific.

For example, if you feel weak in the area of human anatomy and physiology, you may not be able to afford a college course or a workshop. Or maybe you simply do not have the time. Instead, you could purchase a book and interactive CD-ROM. If you wish to learn more about a specific topic, such as how to use an agility ladder, you can purchase a DVD on this specific topic instead of having to attend a seminar that includes all types of other information.

While you cannot obtain CEUs by reading books or watching videos, they are a great way to improve yourself and your business. Personal trainers who take advantage of these resources will have better success keeping their programs safe, fresh, and exciting.

Drawbacks to In-Home Learning

Because you are learning at home, you do not have the benefit of an instructor who can answer questions. Correspondence courses are sometimes the exception. This may not be an issue if the course is fairly straightforward, but if you are truly struggling, you will have to seek help elsewhere. You may be able to find another trainer who can assist you, but this begins to negate the convenience factor.

Because you do not receive hands-on, practical experience, there will be some instances where you may need to supplement your in-home learning with workshops. For topics such as nutrition, basic anatomy, or business, this is not an issue. However, learning new exercises or techniques with only the guidance of a book or video can be a challenge.

Many times, companies offering home-study courses will send you a course catalog with information detailing what you will learn from what they offer. They may sound quite enticing on paper, and you may feel tempted to order multiple courses. Keep in mind, however, that while you may have the best intentions of completing the courses you order, you may not finish them. When you are not required to do the work at a certain time, you will be more likely to procrastinate. When you attend a workshop, you have to be there at a predesignated time, so getting there is half of the battle. It is easier for life to get in the way of your in-home learning. Cleaning the house, cooking dinner, or your favorite television show may end up taking precedence over your professional development.

Continuing-Education Providers

There are so many continuing-education providers and means of obtaining CEUs that choosing a provider can feel overwhelming. This is a very important decision, because you are spending your hard-earned money and deserve to get your money's worth. Some providers will try to bombard you with marketing, so you choose to spend your money with them. Be sure that whatever provider you use meets your needs, and if you need CEUs, be sure it is approved by your certifying agency.

 Fact

IDEA Health and Fitness Association (✑www.ideafit.com) offers a great selection of educational products and seminars, as do the catalog-based equipment suppliers Perform Better, Power Systems, and SPRI Fitness. Human Kinetics (✑www.humankinetics.com) publishes a vast array of books for use by health and fitness professionals in addition to offering online courses.

Your Certifying Organization

Maintaining your certification will cost money. Check with your certifying organization to see what they offer in terms of continuing education units. They will likely offer discounted prices to their members, and you are assured that these credits will count toward your certification. Most organizations offer home-study courses, seminars and workshops, and journal quizzes.

Preapproved Providers

Any medium that teaches you something you did not know before is continuing education. However, that does not necessarily mean that it will qualify for continuing education units toward your recertification. If you are going to spend the time and money on professional development, you would be wise to make sure it can also be counted toward your CEUs.

E ssential

Just because something is not approved for CEUs, does not mean it is not worth doing. There will be times when a course or workshop will offer you valuable insight and experience, and you should not rule it out simply because you cannot receive credit for it. Consider the cost and benefits before making your final decision.

Each organization has a list of continuing-education providers from whom they will accept credits. This is to ensure that the credits represent a quality educational experience and that they are applicable to your certification. When you receive information about a continuing education program, the agencies that accept the credits should be listed on the bottom. You may be able to submit credits from a provider who is not on your agency's list. However, this is something you need to get approved ahead of time so you are not wasting valuable time and money. When in doubt, always ask. It only takes a minute to send an e-mail or make a phone call. You are a valued member of your certifying agency, and will be treated as such.

Cautionary Notes

Continuing education should be taken very seriously. It is not simply an obligation to be filled; it is an opportunity to grow as a health and fitness professional. Through continuing education, you can work at making your weaknesses into strengths, learn new skills, and improve on skills you already have.

Step Out of Your Comfort Zone

Do not limit yourself when it comes to obtaining CEUs. You may be tempted to stay within the areas where you are comfortable because it is easier and safer. But you will gain so much more by stepping out of the box and challenging yourself.

If you continue to acquire knowledge only in the areas in which you are strong, you will be neglecting your weaknesses. It would be more beneficial to obtain the majority of your CEUs in areas where you are not as strong or as comfortable. That is not to say you should not improve on your areas of interest; just do not ignore the areas needing improvement.

 **Alert**

If you tested a client and found weak muscles, you would spend most of your time strengthening those areas to correct imbalances. If instead you continued to work on the muscles that were normal and neglected the weaknesses, your client would never reach their full potential. You can think of your continuing education as being those weak muscles.

The more areas you can become proficient in, the better you can serve your clients and the more diverse your services will be. If you are afraid to branch out into other areas, you could be missing out on a significant portion of the personal-training market.

Choosing a Certifying Organization Based on CEUs

Sometimes aspiring trainers are tempted to become certified by an agency that requires a lesser amount of continuing education. Their thinking is that they will save time and money, but this is not a sound philosophy. The truth is, the more reputable organizations require more CEUs because they value education and want their trainers to be the best in the industry. Taking the easy way out is a huge mistake. You can put yourself and your clients at risk if you do not have sufficient knowledge and background.

Chapter 20

Preparing for the Future

Now is the perfect time to have or begin a personal-training business. The industry is booming in popularity and growth, and shows no signs of slowing down. With so many people wanting and needing the services of personal trainers, qualified trainers are almost guaranteed to make a good living. Ask yourself, though, if you want to make a good living, or grow a huge business. If mediocrity is unacceptable, you must take very specific, well-thought-out steps to nurture and grow your business to greatness.

The Future of the Personal Training Industry

Understanding the industry is critical to positioning yourself for growth and success. Just as the stereotypical personal trainer of ten years ago would not be successful in the market today, you, too could become outdated if you do not keep up with the rapid changes that are taking place. Successful businesses are those that make educated predictions about the future of their industry by looking at present trends. By being aware of and involved in the huge changes taking place, you cannot only keep up with the industry, you can set the pace!

Standardization of Certification

There are likely to be some major changes in the industry in the coming years. Education is becoming more of an emphasis and priority, and those with inadequate education will be left behind. As with physical therapy and athletic training, people are pushing for government regulation of the profession and legal standards for those who can call themselves personal trainers. This will require a national certification exam and state licensure requirements. It is widely believed within the industry that this will bring more credibility to the profession. This will also decrease the escalating numbers of organizations that offer certifications and limit them to offering continuing education. This is yet another reason to be sure you are certified through a reputable organization.

Eventually, every personal trainer will be required to have a college degree in a related field and a certain amount of hands-on experience before they can become certified. The result will be more qualified, safer, and more professional trainers. This may also prompt the development of assistant personal-trainer certifications. If this does occur, assistant trainers would not be required to have as much education. They would probably perform tasks such as prescreening or stretching, but would not be able to create programs for clients.

 Fact

Because of the appealing hours and good compensation, there are an increasing number of physical therapists and athletic trainers choosing to become personal trainers. This raises the bar, as people in the allied health professions are highly educated, are qualified to work with special populations, and have a great deal of hands-on experience.

Teaming Up with the Health-Care Industry

Insurance companies already acknowledge that personal training is preventative health care, and that for every $1 spent on prevention they save about $10 on treatment. That is why many insurance companies will now reimburse their members for part or all of a gym membership. In the future, they may also reimburse for the services of personal trainers, which would make training more affordable and more appealing to the average person.

The medical field as a whole is also recognizing the importance of prevention and the benefits for their patients of working with a personal trainer. They are also realizing that reciprocal relationships with trainers can help their businesses be more successful. There is an increasing amount of cooperation between the medical and fitness industries in the effort to increase the number of people living healthy lifestyles. Personal trainers are aligning more and more with doctors, physical therapists, chiropractors, and other medical professionals, opening up another market.

Alert

The leading and most respected organizations are ACSM, NSCA, and NASM. If you want to be prepared for the impending changes in the industry, obtain a certification with one of these organizations. If personal training is more of a hobby or part-time job, one of the other organizations listed in Chapter 1 will be sufficient.

What Do These Changes Mean?

Any and all of these changes will increase respect and demand for personal-training services. With an increase in demand comes an increase in compensation. Personal trainers as a group will be more educated, better qualified, and more professional. People will be willing to pay more because they know they are getting more. However, if you want to be a part of this exciting growth, you need to have adequate education and a respected certification.

More and more colleges and universities are recognizing personal training as a viable career for the future. They are offering degrees in personal training that enable their students to become certified through a reputable organization, as well as providing them hands-on experience and training. If this interests you (and it should), it should be relatively easy to find a college in your area that offers this type of degree. If you obtain this level of education, you will be prepared for the time when there is a national certification exam and state licensure for personal trainers; you will not have to scramble to get the proper schooling after the fact. You will also be contributing to the growing level of professionalism within the industry.

Providing New Services

Expanding the services you offer will help you reach populations that do not typically do business with you. It will also provide your current members with added benefits and will give them the opportunity to increase the amount of business they do with you. Consider the services you already provide and who is using them. What else could you offer that would draw new people in and also benefit your current clients? By making educated decisions based on what people want and need, you will be able to gain more of the market share in your community. This will in turn increase revenue and help you grow your business. Trainers who have their own facilities will have more options because they have more space. However, independent trainers also have quite a few options for offering additional services to their clients, especially when they can be creative.

Expanding Your Market

If you want your business to experience dramatic growth, you'll have to attract people from different markets. How will you know where to expand your business or what niche will allow you to develop more business? Keep a finger on the pulse of the fitness industry by reading trade magazines and going to trade shows and seminars. Examine the new trends or growing needs of the population in your part of the country. Survey your clients and ask them what they want or need that you are currently not providing. Survey people who are not currently clients to determine what services you could offer to attract them. Be prepared to offer programs and services in the future that you are currently not offering. Try to predict and stay one step ahead of the latest trends; your business model should be proactive, not reactive. If you are the first trainer in the area providing this new service, you will capture most of the business as the service gets more popular.

Specialization

More and more trainers are settling into a niche or specialty. People are opening their own facilities and specializing in all kinds of things: sports performance training, weight management, rehabilitation, etc. The days when trainers worked only in gyms and with healthy populations are gone. Having a specialization will set you apart from other trainers and can give you an edge. This will typically require you to obtain additional education or certifications. Health clubs are looking to hire highly educated trainers who can attract and work with the postrehabilitation market.

Get Creative with Your Talents

Think about what you enjoy and are good at besides personal training. If you are a fabulous cook, perhaps you can offer to cook healthy meals for your clients for a weekly fee. You could also offer healthy-cooking classes for small groups of people. Or maybe you want to add a café or juice bar in your facility. If motivation is your strong suit, try putting together support groups for your clients and other people in the community who share common goals, such as weight loss. The possibilities are unlimited. Not only can you make extra money, you will get your name out there and may attract new clients as well.

Offering Total Wellness

There is a growing trend toward obtaining health in all areas of life: physical, spiritual, mental, and emotional. While personal trainers typically focus on physical improvements, there is a great deal of potential in addressing the other areas as well. Offering wellness alternatives will create new business opportunities for your future. There are many ways to take advantage of the increasingly popular movement.

Wellness Centers

Wellness centers combine the services of medical and fitness personnel with the goal of helping people achieve total health. In addition to the services traditionally offered by health clubs, wellness centers may offer services such as weight-loss counseling, smoking-cessation classes, or rehabilitation. Some integrate holistic and alternative therapies to treat stress and chronic diseases like diabetes. By doing so, they attract a more diverse group of members. They are able to attend to their clients' needs more completely than health clubs or gyms. Each center is unique in scope and practice, so it is up to you to find or establish a center that fits your belief system.

Alternative Health Options

If opening or working in a wellness center does not interest you or is not a possibility at this time, you could obtain additional certifications that will allow you to offer more wellness services. Yoga, Pilates, meditation, Reiki, massage therapy, and other nontraditional exercises or therapies can be great complements to personal training. They can help your clients reduce stress and feel more balanced. Some will require more time and money to earn certifications, so make sure you understand what type of commitment you are making.

 Question

With so many supplements on the market, how do I know which to sell?
Do your research so you feel comfortable with the safety and quality of the products you sell. The nutritional-supplement industry is largely unregulated, and many products are ineffective or even unsafe. Consumerlab.com performs independent research and lists companies that pass their tests on their site. This is a great place to begin your research.

In order to practice these specialties, you will need a quiet, private space to designate for these uses. If you do not have the space available, you can travel to your clients' homes and work with them individually, or with small groups of their friends. If you do have the space available and can work out the logistics, it will be worth the effort. Your clients will appreciate the variety and convenience, and they may help you attract people who otherwise would not be interested in what you offer.

Wellness Coaching

Wellness coaching, also called life coaching, is an up-and-coming profession. It began in the eighties and is rapidly increasing in popularity. Wellness coaches are specifically trained to help people overcome barriers to success. They are professional motivators and mentors. As a trainer, a huge part of what you are doing is coaching your clients. Becoming certified as a wellness coach can improve the services you provide your clients, enable you to charge a higher hourly rate, and attract new clientele. If you would like to investigate this certification, you can log on to ✐*www.spencerinstitute.com.*

Selling Nutritional Supplements

Nutrition and nutritional supplements are part of total wellness. They can be used for weight loss, stress relief, heart health, and more. When used properly, supplements can be a great tool to help your clients reach their goals. On a daily basis, you are meeting with people who want to lose weight, build muscle, and feel better. They already trust your judgment and will likely do as you say, within reason. People are buying these products anyway, so why not let them buy them from you? You can better supervise what they are doing, and you know they are using good-quality products.

 Fact

The U.S. population spends over $30 billion a year on health and fitness products. You are in a position to capitalize on this fact. You have a captive audience who is already looking to you to address their health and fitness. Why not supplement your income by giving people what they are looking for?

There are many companies who supply supplements at wholesale costs. You purchase energy drinks, recovery drinks, protein bars, and vitamins, and then resell them at retail prices. For tax purposes, you will need a resale license in order to do this. Your clients will appreciate the convenience factor of being able to grab something on their way out.

If you do not have a place to keep inventory or do not want to obtain a resale license, you can use a network-marketing company. Shaklee Corporation (*www.shaklee.com*) is the most reputable nutritional-supplement company in the network-marketing industry. Your customers can purchase their all-natural supplements from you, or can buy direct from the company. Either way, you are credited with and compensated for the sale every time. If you have enough of your clients purchasing these products every month, you can generate thousands of dollars in income.

Online Training

You cannot open a trade magazine or attend a conference where the Internet and Web-based training are not discussed. Doing business on the Internet is becoming increasingly popular. It is an inexpensive way to reach large numbers of people, and is a great way to leverage your time. People spend hours on their computers, making the Internet a great way to interact with present and potential clients. Over the coming years, Web-based training will likely increase in popularity and offer even more services. If you miss out on this wave of the future, you are limiting the potential growth of your business.

Web-Based Training

Web-based training involves either developing your own site, or subscribing to a pre-existing site in order to provide your clients with programs. You may choose to create your own site, but this is not really time or cost effective. For a small monthly fee, you can purchase subscription-based programs that allow you to offer much more. When you open an account with companies like Trainer Force or Fitness Generator, you will be able to:

- Create customized questionnaires and assessments
- Track your clients' workouts
- Create customized workouts and meal plans
- Keep clients current on the latest fitness research
- Link to your own Web site

You then give your clients a password so they can:

- Fill out the questionnaires
- Set goals
- View your customized programs
- See clips of the exercises being performed
- Log workouts

These services are available for $40–$50 per month and will allow you to train a significantly greater number of clients, as well as provide better service to the clients you already have. As Web-based training grows in popularity, there are an increasing number of companies offering this service. Due to competition, they are continually improving the services and benefits they offer and can help you generate a great deal of income if you utilize them properly.

Alert

If you do choose to offer online training, it is wise to require an in-person consultation when possible. This will allow you to perform your complete fitness assessment and establish rapport with your clients. You can get to know people much more intimately when you meet face to face.

Complementing Your Business with Online Training

Online training by itself can help you earn money. However, it is less effective alone than when you use it as a complement to your traditional training. Most people need the human component of support and accountability in order to stick with their programs and be successful. You can use your Web site to have your clients obtain their programs and log their workouts, and you can then require them to meet with you at regular intervals to check in. You can do it over the phone, but face-to-face meetings are best.

Personal training is more affordable for people when they only have to meet with you once or twice a month. Instead of training with you one to two times per week and spending $400 per month, they will pay $50 for the session with you and an additional $25–$50 for the Web service. A lot more people will be willing to pay $100 a month than they will be to pay $400. As a result, a greater number of people will utilize your services. You will also be freed up to help a larger number of people in the same amount of time you were working before.

E ssential

You might consider using your in-person meetings to perform exercise testing. This will allow you to truly measure progress and see if the programs have been effective. You can also take this time to evaluate and modify goals as necessary, or address any problems or concerns your clients may have.

Love Training Over the Long Haul

Personal training is anything but easy. You must continually sell in order to maintain a full schedule. The hours can be long, and you must always be on top of your game. Having a bad day is not an option. You spend your time listening to and trying to solve problems, whether they are physical, mental, or emotional. After a while, you can become exhausted, overwhelmed, or even bored. The rewards of working as a personal trainer are tremendous, but if you do not take the proper steps, you can find yourself no longer enjoying your career. If you stop enjoying what you are doing, you will not be able to grow personally or professionally. If you stop loving what you do, burnout and the end of your career could be just around the corner.

Keeping It Fresh

One way to prevent burnout is to continuously increase your knowledge base. Expanding your understanding of different aspects of the industry will help you prevent boredom in a number of ways. First, it will allow you to work with a variety of people and ability levels. You will not be taking your clients through the same types of workouts all of the time. Personal training, just like any job, will have a certain level of redundancy. If you do not challenge yourself, you could easily end up performing exactly the same tasks, the same way, day in and day out. Gaining knowledge can empower you to take charge of your career and try new things.

Alert

Limiting the amount of time you spend training is one way to avoid burnout. Have designated times where you will and will not work and stick to them. Create a life for yourself outside of the gym. Make time for your family, your friends, and your hobbies. If you want to love your career for the long haul, take a break!

Attending seminars and conferences will help keep you motivated and excited about your career. You will learn new things from presenters, as well as the other trainers in attendance. Take the opportunity to exchange information and ideas with the people you meet. Ask them to share with you their successes and failures, as well as how they stay excited about what they are doing.

There Is More to Life

Carefully watch over the hours you keep. With the high hourly rate for personal trainers, it is easy to get caught up in working extra hours. You can end up overloading your schedule and working more and more, until you feel you have no control over what is happening. Every minute you spend with your clients you have to be "on." It is not the kind of job where you can hide behind your desk when you need a break. Your clients need you to motivate them and to be vigilant about their safety. Your energy and enthusiasm must remain high at all times. This is draining over the course of a day. When you work extra-long days, it is even worse, because you have no downtime. Work becomes drudgery instead of being enjoyable, and by the time you realize you are sick of the grind, you may already be suffering from burnout.

Taking time for yourself during the workday can help you keep your energy up. Stop for a lunch or dinner break just as you would for any other job. Because your clients may use their lunch breaks for exercise, you may need to take yours a little earlier or a little later, but do not skip it. You need time to sit down, recharge, and gather your thoughts. This will allow you to give just as much to your clients during the second half of your day as you do to your clients in the beginning of your day.

You Deserve a Vacation

If you are an independent trainer, taking time off for vacation can be a difficult choice to make. You will not be paid during the time you are away, so you may lose a significant amount of money. However, if you do not take time for rest and recovery you are doing yourself and your clients a disservice. It is not possible to perform at peak capacity for endless periods of time. Making money is nice, but part of being an example of health is living a balanced lifestyle. Taking time off will decrease your stress levels and you will return more motivated and focused than before. This renewed energy and focus will make you a better personal trainer.

Keeping Your Distance/Establishing Boundaries

Because you are continuously trying to uncover barriers to your clients' success, you will constantly hear about their problems. Listen to what they are saying only to the extent of using the information to help them progress; do not make your clients' problems your own. Most personal trainers enter the profession because they want to help people, but it is possible to nurture too much. If you take your clients' troubles as your own, you will burnout emotionally. Just remember that you cannot solve every issue—it's up to your clients to help themselves. Protect yourself from the perils of taking on too much by focusing on what you are being paid for; implementing a safe and effective exercise program.

Appendix A

Medical Forms and Questionnaires

Health Questionnaire

Name: _____ Date: _____

Address: _____ Age: ____ DOB: _____

City: _____ State: ___ Sex: __ Weight: _____

Zip: _____ E-mail: _____

Home #: _____ Business #: _____ Cell #: _____

Emergency contact: _____ Phone #: _____

Physician name: _____ Phone #: _____

Address: _____

Date and reason last consulted: _____

1. Has your physician ever advised you against exercising?

   Yes ❑   No ❑

   If yes, please explain: _____

   _____

2. Do you know or have you ever experienced any of the following:

Chest pains	Yes ❏	No ❏	Daily coughing	Yes ❏	No ❏
Chest pressure	Yes ❏	No ❏	Fainting	Yes ❏	No ❏
Palpitations/ Skipped beats	Yes ❏	No ❏	Seizures	Yes ❏	No ❏
Unexplained weight change	Yes ❏	No ❏	Shortness of breath when exercising	Yes ❏	No ❏
Numbness or tingling	Yes ❏	No ❏	Allergies	Yes ❏	No ❏
Stumbling	Yes ❏	No ❏	Difficulty walking	Yes ❏	No ❏
Frequent headaches	Yes ❏	No ❏	Dizziness	Yes ❏	No ❏

3. Do you have or did a physician ever diagnose you as having any of the following:

Heart disease	Yes ❏	No ❏	Diabetes	Yes ❏	No ❏
Heart murmur	Yes ❏	No ❏	Emphysema	Yes ❏	No ❏
Arrhythmia	Yes ❏	No ❏	Asthma	Yes ❏	No ❏
Circulatory problems	Yes ❏	No ❏	Chronic bronchitis	Yes ❏	No ❏
High blood pressure	Yes ❏	No ❏	Neurological problems	Yes ❏	No ❏
High cholesterol	Yes ❏	No ❏	Arthritis	Yes ❏	No ❏
Osteoporosis	Yes ❏	No ❏	Cancer	Yes ❏	No ❏

Condition(s) not listed: _____

_____

4. Are you presently under a physician's care for any of the above, or any other condition?

   Yes ❏   No ❏

   If yes, please explain. _____

   _____

5. Have you had any major illnesses and/or surgeries?

   Yes ❏   No ❏

   If yes, please explain. _____

   _____

6. Do you have any current medical problems or incompletely healed injuries?

   Yes ❏   No ❏

   If yes, please explain. _____

   _____

7. Have you had or do you now have any bone, joint (including spine), or muscle injuries or diseases?

   Yes ❏   No ❏

   If yes, please explain. _____

   _____

8. Are you presently receiving physical therapy?

   Yes ❏   No ❏

   If yes, please explain. _____

   _____

9. Is there any position, activity, exercise, or task that causes you concern or pain?

Yes ❏   No ❏

If yes, please explain. _____

_____

10. In what way do your symptoms interfere with your daily activities?

_____

_____

11. If you do experience any pain or discomfort, what causes the symptoms?

_____

_____

12. Are you presently taking medications? Please list dosage and reason.

_____

_____

Providing your signature will indicate that all of the information provided above is true to the best of your knowledge. That_____

Company name_____will be notified if and when there are any physical or mental conditions that may affect physical activity.

Name: _____ Sign: _____

Date: _____

Informed Consent

I, _____ understand the potential risks involved in participating in a rigorous physical exercise program.

I assume the responsibility and risks as explained to me. I understand that participating in an exercise program may include, but not be limited to, serious bodily injury, heart attack, stroke, or even death.

I consent voluntarily to participate in an exercise program based on the information provided to me.

Name: _____

Signature: _____

Date: _____

Witness: _____

Liability Waiver Form

I, _____, certify and acknowledge:

That _____ Company name _____

_____, an independent personal trainer, has advised me prior to my commencement of participation in cardiovascular and resistance training programs that such participation could result in physical injury.

That I,_____, freely and knowingly assume the risk in such programs, and I hereby waive any right, claim, or cause of action against _____ Company name _____ and release him/her and/or his/her company from any liability for any injury, cost, damage expense or claim, which I or anyone on my behalf might incur as a direct or indirect result of my participation in this cardiovascular and resistance-training program.

That I,_____, have read this Liability Waiver form, understand and agree with each of the foregoing points, and have received a copy of this release form on this date.

Print Name: _____

Signature: _____

Date: _____

Medical Release Form

Date: _____

Dear Doctor _____:

My Client, _____ has hired me as their personal trainer and named you as their primary health care provider. They would like to start a cardiovascular and/or resistance-training program. The program will involve the following:

Type of exercise: _____
Frequency: _____
Duration: _____
Intensity level of exercise: _____

Please identify any medication that will affect their heart rate and/or blood pressure.

Type of medication: _____
Effects of medication: _____

Please give any instructions or restrictions pertaining to your client participating in an exercise program.

_____

_____

Clients name: _____has been approved to begin an exercise program following the guidelines provided.

Doctor's signature: _____ Date: _____

Phone: _____ Fax: _____

Thank you,

Your name _____

Contact information _____

Accident Report

DATE: _____

TIME: _____
LOCATION: _____

CLAIMANT INFORMATION:
Member _____ or Non-member _____
NAME: _____
ADDRESS: _____
_____
TEL. #: _____ DOB: _____

DESCRIPTION OF ACCIDENT/INJURY:
_____
_____
_____
_____

WITNESSES: _____

Witnesses' Contact Information: _____

Emergency personnel called? Yes _____ No _____

First Aid administered? Yes _____ No _____

COMMENTS:
_____
_____
_____

Instructor/Personal Trainer: _____

Copy to insurance company: Yes _____ No _____

Equipment Suppliers

Balanced Body Pilates

✍ *www.pilates.com*

800-745-2837

Ball Dynamics International, LLC

✍ *www.fitball.com*

800-752-2255

C.H.E.K. Institute

✍ *www.chekinstitute.com*

800-552-8789

The Core Spinal Fitness System by MedX

✍ *www.corespinalfitness.com*

866-814-0719

FreeMotion Fitness

✍ *www.freemotionfitness.com*

877-363-8449

Fundamental Fitness Products, Inc.

✍ *www.funfitpro.com*

866-207-6308

Trainer's Wholesale

✍ *www.trainerswholesale.com*

323-931-2902

JP Design and Manufacturing, Inc.

✍ *www.jpdesignandmfg.com*

866-917-8776

Perform Better

✍ *www.performbetter.com*

888-556-7464

Power Systems, Inc.

✍ *www.power-systems.com*

800-321-6975

Vortex Fitness Equipment LLC

✍ *www.vortexfitness.com*

877-676-4677

Heart-rate Monitors

Cardiosport
✍ www.cardiosport.com

Casio
✍ www.casio.com

Heart Monitors
✍ www.heartmonitor.com

Heart Zones
✍ www.heartzone.com

Polar
✍ www.polar.com

Timex Ironman
✍ www.timex.com

Appendix C

Additional Resources

Here are some organizations, publications, and Web sites that can help you learn more about personal training.

Certifying Agencies

American College of Sports Medicine (ACSM)
✍ *www.acsm.org*

National Strength and Conditioning Association (NSCA)
✍ *www.nsca.com*

National Academy of Sports Medicine (NASM)
✍ *www.nasm.org*

American Council on Exercise (ACE)
✍ *www.acefitness.org*

Aerobics and Fitness Association of America (AFAA)
✍ *www.afaa.com*

National Federation of Personal Trainers (NFPT)
✍ *www.nfpt.com*

National Council on Strength and Fitness (NCSF)
✍ *www.ncsf.org*

International Sports Sciences Association (ISSA)
✍ *www.issaonline.com*

American Fitness Professionals & Associates (AFPA)
✍ *www.afpafitness.com*

National Exercise and Sports Trainers Association (NESTA)
✍ *www.nestacertified.com*

National Organization for Competency Assurance (NOCA)
✍ *www.noca.org*

Business Help

Business.gov (Official business link to U.S. government)
✍ *www.business.gov*

Inc.
✍ *www.inc.com*

AllBusiness.com
✍ *www.allbusiness.com*

Small Business Association (SBA)
✍ *www.sba.gov*

Chamber of Commerce
✍ *www.uschamber.com*

IRS
✍ *www.irs.gov*

BNI
✍ *www.bni.com*

Business Plan Software
✍ *www.bplans.com*

Continuing Education

IDEA Health and Fitness Association
✍ *www.ideafit.com*

Human Kinetics
✍ *www.humankinetics.com*

Perform Better
✍ *www.performbetter.com*

Power Systems
✍ *www.power-systems.com*

SPRI Fitness
✍ *www.spriproducts.com*

Journals, Magazines, and Books

Strength and Conditioning Journal
Published by the National Strength and Conditioning Association Bi-monthly. Publishes articles on the latest research findings and knowledge of experienced professionals in the field. (80 pages)

Journal of Strength and Conditioning Research
Quarterly publication of the National Strength and Conditioning Association that prints original research by strength and conditioning experts.(120 pages)
✍ *www.nsca-lift.org/publications*

Personal Fitness Professional

Provides business information for personal trainers, from education to how to earn more money while improving their services.

✐ *www.fit-pro.com*

ClubSolutions Magazine

Geared toward the owner/general manager of health and fitness establishments.

✐ *www.clubsolutionsmagazine .com*

502-254-7021

Fitness

✐ *www.fitness.com*

Men's Health

✐ *www.menshealth.com*

Self

✐ *www.self.com*

Shape

✐ *www.shape.com*

Encyclopedia of Muscle & Strength by Jim Stoppani

This research-based book gets a little technical, but if you want to truly understand the principles behind building muscle and strength as well as have an in-depth look at the muscles and what they do, this book is a great resource. It also includes exercises and workout programs designed to build mass and strength.

Strength Training Past 50 by Wayne L. Westcott and Thomas R. Baechle

This book is a great resource for exercisers in their fifties and older. The authors discuss the reasons that strength training is so important, especially for seniors, and offers strength tests as well as programs to increase strength and endurance.

YOU: The Owner's Manual by Michael F. Roizen and Mehmet Oz

This easy-to-read book covers every part of the human body, from how your thyroid works to basic anatomy and physiology of the human body. It also includes a food plan and guidelines for a basic exercise program.

Eating Thin for Life: Food Secrets & Recipes from People Who Have Lost Weight & Kept It Off by Anne M. Fletcher

The best advice you can get is sometimes from real people who've managed to lose weight and keep it off. This book offers the experiences of over 200 people who have created and maintained healthy lifestyles.

Business Software

Twin Oaks   *www.tosd.com*

eFit Financial   *www.efitfinancial.com*

ABC Financial   *www.abcfinancial.com*

ASF International   *www.asfint.com*

CSI Software   *www.csisoftwareusa.com*

Web Sites of Interest

About.com Bodybuilding

You don't have to be a body-builder to appreciate Hugo Rivera's site. He offers great information about building muscle, losing fat, and beginning a strength-training program.
http://bodybuilding.about.com

About.com Exercise

Paige Waehner, the About.com guide to exercise, is an ACE-certified personal trainer who trains clients in their homes in the Chicago area. Her site includes information on nutrition, cardiovascular training, weight training, supplements, and more.
http://exercise.about.com

About.com Nutrition

Shereen Jegtvig's Nutrition site offers a wealth of information about the basics of nutrition. Here you'll find information you can pass onto your clients about low-carb diets, essential nutrients your body needs, and more.
http://nutrition.about.com

About.com Pilates

Marguerite Ogle's Pilates site provides detailed information about Pilates. You'll learn about the principles behind Pilates, how to breathe during Pilates exercises, how to find a good teacher, and basic Pilates exercises.
http://pilates.about.com

About.com Pregnancy/Birth

Are you training clients who are pregnant or postpartum? If so you may be interested in learning more about healthy pregnancy as well as what your pregnant client can expect at every point during their pregnancy. Visit Robin Elise Weiss's Pregnancy site. She offers articles and tips for prenatal health, postpartum issues, and more.
http://pregnancy.about.com

About.com Running/Jogging

Whether you want to help your clients run a marathon or just make it around the block, Jesslyn Cummings can help you figure out where to start, with articles, step-by-step guides, shoe reviews, and free running programs.
http://running.about.com

About.com Sports Medicine

Whether you are training in a gym, at home, or outdoors, you'll find great information at Elizabeth Quinn's Sports Medicine site. She covers the ins and outs of sports injuries, the basics of strength training, and how to get the most out of your body no matter what activities you're involved in.
http://sportsmedicine.about. com

About.com Walking Guide

Wendy Bumgardner's Walking site should be your first stop if you'd like to start a walking program for your clients. She has a number of free walking programs and workouts as well as information about tools, clothing, shoes, and more.
http://walking.about.com

About.com Weight Loss

Jennifer R. Scott's Weight Loss site offers great information about losing weight, including tips for beginners, detailed articles about specific diets, and information on exercise.
http://weightloss.about.com

About.com Yoga

If you'd like to learn more about yoga, especially how to do a variety of yoga postures, visit Ann Pizer's site. She has an extensive database and photo gallery of yoga poses as well as great information about how to get started and which type of yoga is best for you.
http://yoga.about.com

American Council on Exercise Library

If you're looking for new and interesting exercise ideas, ACE offers an extensive library that includes everything from balance and stability moves to yoga and strength-training exercises.
www.acefitness.org/getfit/ freeexercise.aspx

Calorie Control Council

This site offers information about how your clients can cut calories in their diets to lose weight and get healthy. There are a variety of tools like calorie

and activity calculators as well as a wealth of recipes and articles about eating healthy.
✍ *www.caloriecontrol.org*

ExRx.net
This site offers a wealth of information about exercise, fitness, and nutrition. They have an extensive database of exercises as well as information about exercise guidelines, strength training, cardio exercise, and more.
✍ *www.exrx.net*

Plus One Active
Plus One Active offers a variety of online personal training programs. You can choose to work with a trainer and receive a variety of workouts, or if you're more independent, you can sign up to receive a workout program.
✍ *www.plusoneactive.com*

Workouts for Women
This site offers online personal training programs for women as well as advice on nutrition, weight loss, and fitness.
✍ *www.workoutsforwomen.com*

Index

The Everything® Career Guide Series

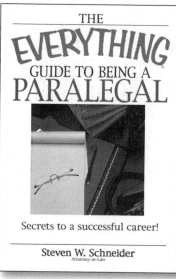

Secrets to a successful career!

Steven W. Schneider
Attorney-at-Law

Trade Paperback, $14.95
ISBN 10: 1-59337-583-2
ISBN 13: 978-1-59337-583-6

Secrets to a successful career!

Shahri Masters
Author of The Everything® Homeselling Book, 2nd Edition

Trade Paperback, $14.95
ISBN 10: 1-59337-432-1
ISBN 13: 978-1-59337-432-7

Winning secrets to a successful–
and profitable–career!

Ruth Klein

Trade Paperback, $14.95
ISBN 10: 1-59337-657-X
ISBN 13: 978-1-59337-657-4

Secrets to a successful business!

Ronald Lee, Restaurateur

Trade Paperback, $14.95
ISBN 10: 1-59337-433-X
ISBN 13: 978-1-59337-433-4

Helpful handbooks written by experts.

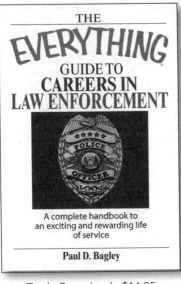